THEGREATWAR100
THE FIRST WORLD WAR IN INFOGRAPHICS

SCOTT ADDINGTON

The
History
Press ▶

ACKNOWLEDGEMENTS

Putting together this many infographics has, not surprisingly, been time consuming and at times quite complicated. I could not have done this without John Pring and the team at Designbysoap.

I must also say a big thank you to my wonderful wife, Veronika, who has been incredibly patient and understanding throughout this project.

First published 2014

The History Press
The Mill, Brimscombe Port
Stroud, Gloucestershire, GL5 2QG
www.thehistorypress.co.uk

© Scott Addington, 2014

The right of Scott Addington to be identified as the Author of this work has been asserted in accordance with the Copyrights, Designs and Patents Act 1988.

British Library Cataloguing in Publication Data.
A catalogue record for this book is available from the British Library.

ISBN 978 0 7524 8639 0

Typesetting and origination by The History Press

Printed in India

INTRODUCTION

For many people, especially the younger generation, history can seem a bit ... well, dull. The general perception of traditional history books is that they can be old fashioned. Most are not written to engage the normal man or woman in the street and sometimes it seems that the historian authors are just trying to prove how academically superior they are.

Whatever the reason may be, there are many thousands of people that still do not know much about the First World War.

The teaching of history needs to adapt to the modern way and to twenty-first-century tastes. The consumption of information has changed over the years, and as a result the general public is less inclined to read 900-page epics. They are after the history of the world in 140 characters, not intimate, minute detail on every single tiny aspect and factor of the subject.

As a marketer I have used infographics for many years to communicate to various audiences and they have always been a very effective way of getting complicated messages across to people in an easy-to-digest way. And so I embarked on a plan to try to communicate the First World War using nothing but infographics in an attempt to make the subject more appealing and accessible to those who are not inclined to read those 900-page epics.

To build these graphics I have used many different sources for the background facts, and a full list of references can be found at the back of the book. With complicated events such as the First World War there can be many different interpretations of the evidence. For example, casualty rates for each country can vary wildly depending on what book you read. I have tried very hard to ensure the facts behind the graphics are as accurate as possible, but there may be some areas where discrepancies occur and opinions do differ.

Along with some of the great new apps that are available now, and some fantastic new video documentaries, I hope that this project helps to put an up-to-date twist on history telling and encourages more people to find out about such a fascinating and important subject as the First World War.

Enjoy the graphics!

SMA Spring 2014

Prelude To War: June - August 1914

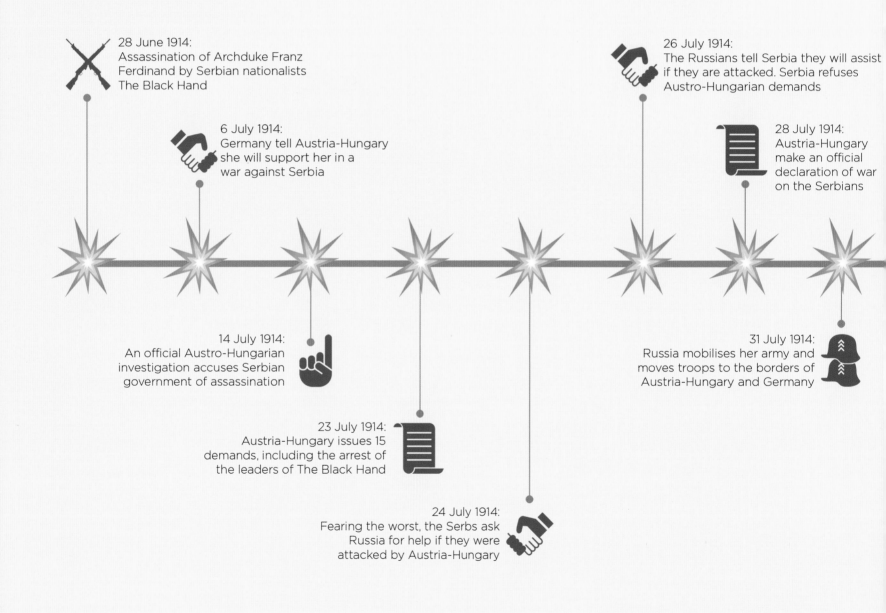

28 June 1914:
Assassination of Archduke Franz Ferdinand by Serbian nationalists The Black Hand

6 July 1914:
Germany tell Austria-Hungary she will support her in a war against Serbia

14 July 1914:
An official Austro-Hungarian investigation accuses Serbian government of assassination

23 July 1914:
Austria-Hungary issues 15 demands, including the arrest of the leaders of The Black Hand

24 July 1914:
Fearing the worst, the Serbs ask Russia for help if they were attacked by Austria-Hungary

26 July 1914:
The Russians tell Serbia they will assist if they are attacked. Serbia refuses Austro-Hungarian demands

28 July 1914:
Austria-Hungary make an official declaration of war on the Serbians

31 July 1914:
Russia mobilises her army and moves troops to the borders of Austria-Hungary and Germany

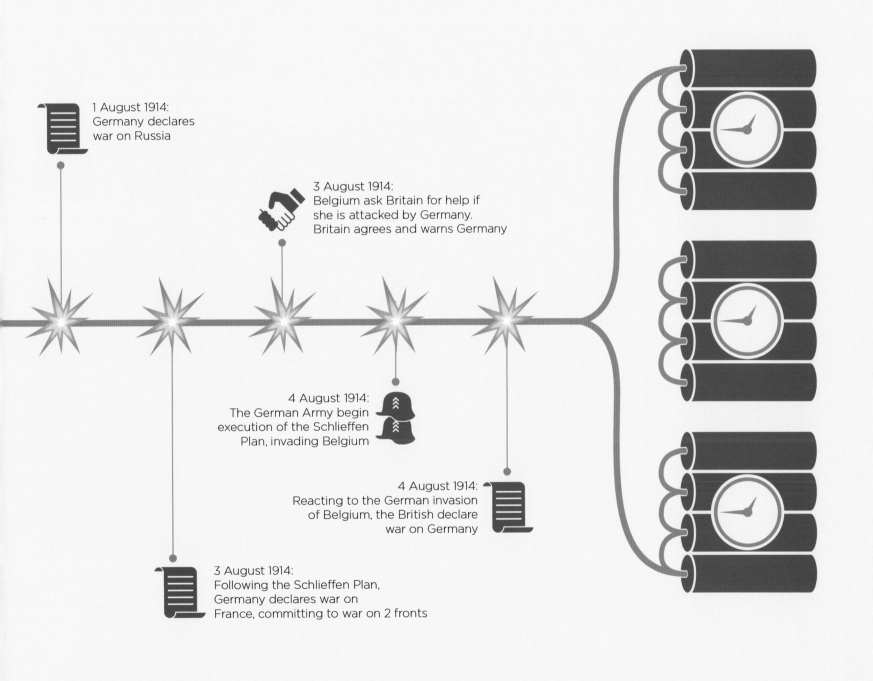

1 August 1914:
Germany declares
war on Russia

3 August 1914:
Belgium ask Britain for help if
she is attacked by Germany.
Britain agrees and warns Germany

4 August 1914:
The German Army begin
execution of the Schlieffen
Plan, invading Belgium

4 August 1914:
Reacting to the German invasion
of Belgium, the British declare
war on Germany

3 August 1914:
Following the Schlieffen Plan,
Germany declares war on
France, committing to war on 2 fronts

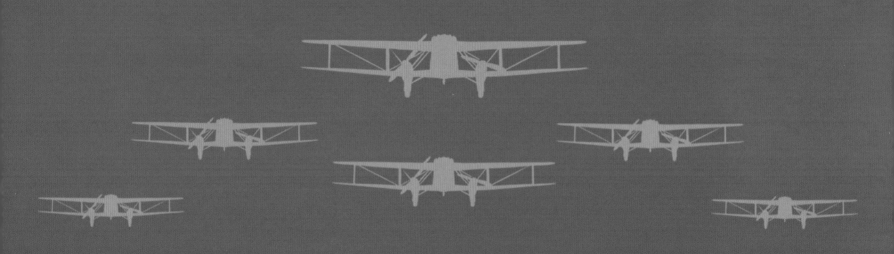

OVERVIEW

By the summer of 1914, some kind of European war had become almost inevitable. The spark that ultimately lit a thousand fires came on the afternoon of 28 June 1914, with the assassination of Archduke Franz Ferdinand in Sarajevo. Exactly one month later Austria-Hungary declared war on Serbia and, by the beginning of August, Europe was split into two very distinct, very powerful and very destructive sides: Austria-Hungary and Germany on one side and Britain, France and Russia on the other.

Popular British sentiment was that the war would be over by Christmas, but the fighting soon bogged down into a static war of attrition and it quickly became apparent that this would be a long, drawn-out conflict.

A war like no other.

The Original Plan

🪖 First drafted by General Count Alfred Von Schlieffen in 1899 to counter the 1892 Franco-Russian alliance.

🪖 Idea was to knock France out of the war before Russia could mobilise her huge army.

🪖 German Army split into two (North and South).

🪖 Northern army to advance through Belgium into France, sweep around Paris and back towards the border.

🪖 Southern army to stay on French border in case of French counter attack.

🪖 Speed of attack critical in achieving success. It was assumed Russia would mobilise within about 6 weeks.

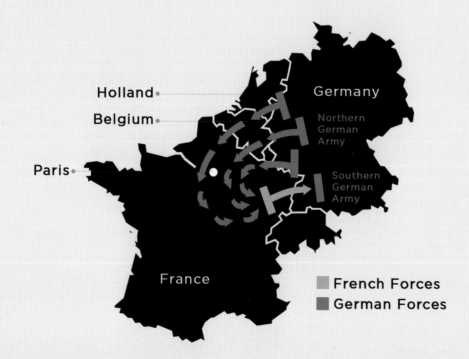

Holland
Belgium
Paris
Germany
Northern German Army
Southern German Army
France

■ French Forces
■ German Forces

PLAN - 1914

The Plan's Reality

- Field Marshal Helmuth von Moltke executed the plan in 1914.

- He was nervous of French counter attacks and moved thousands of troops to the southern army, weakening the fighting force of the north.

- Belgium provided stubborn resistance and slowed the advance.

- Russia mobilised fast and forced the transfer of 85,000 troops away from the advance.

- Continual German advance exhausted the troops and overstretched supply and communication lines.

- The Schlieffen Plan ultimately failed. Paris was saved, but the war was far from over ...

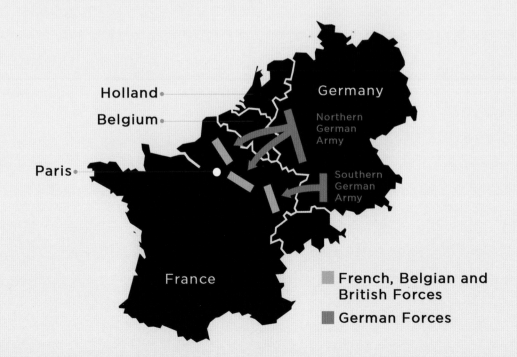

Holland

Belgium

Paris

Germany

Northern German Army

Southern German Army

France

■ French, Belgian and British Forces

■ German Forces

28TH JUNE

ASSASSINATION OF ARCHDUKE FRANZ FERDINAND

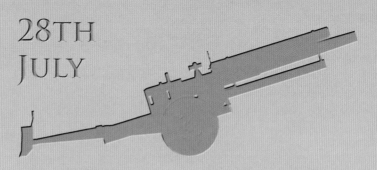

28TH JULY

AUSTRIA-HUNGARY OFFICIALLY DECLARES WAR ON SERBIA

4 MAIN BATTLES

19

—— **MONS** ——
(23RD AUGUST)

—— **MARNE** ——
(6TH SEPTEMBER)

— **TANNENBERG** —
(23RD AUGUST)

—— **FIRST YPRES** ——
(20TH OCTOBER)

4TH AUG

GERMAN FORCES MARCH INTO BELGIUM EN ROUTE TO FRANCE

1ST AUG

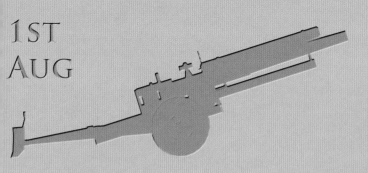

GERMANY OFFICIALLY DECLARES
WAR ON RUSSIA

3RD AUG

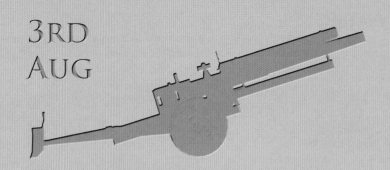

GERMANY OFFICIALLY DECLARES
WAR ON FRANCE

14

4TH AUG

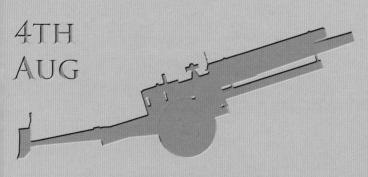

BRITAIN OFFICIALLY DECLARES
WAR ON GERMANY

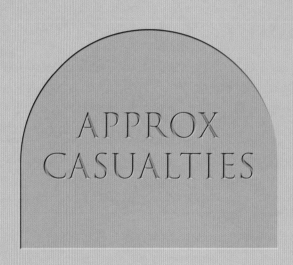

APPROX
CASUALTIES

ALLIED
CASUALTIES
2,943,000

CENTRAL POWERS
CASUALTIES
1,950,000

19TH JAN

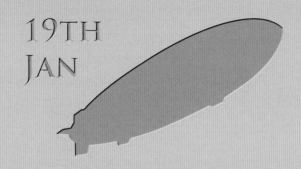

First zeppelin raid on great britain, with 20 casualties

4TH FEB

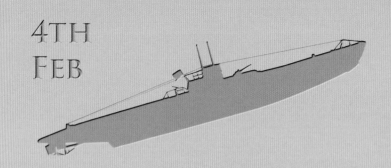

Germany declares unrestricted u-boat war in british waters

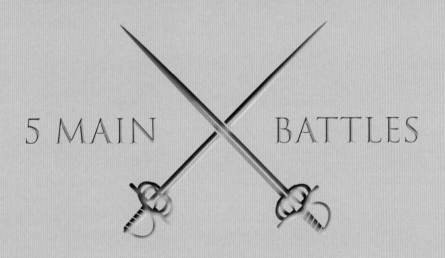

5 MAIN BATTLES

19

NEUVE CHAPPELLE
(10TH MARCH)

GALLIPOLI
(18TH MARCH)

SECOND YPRES
(22ND APRIL)

GORLICE TARNOW
(1ST MAY)

LOOS
(25TH SEPTEMBER)

11TH SEP

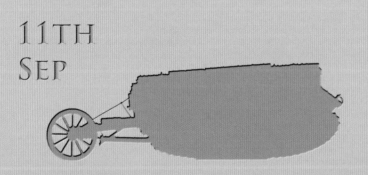

First prototype tank, code-named little willie

22ND APRIL

GERMANY LAUNCHES THE FIRST LARGE-SCALE GAS ATTACK

23RD MAY

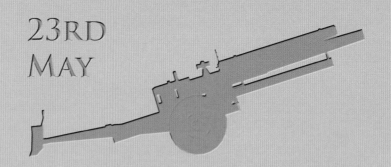

ITALY ENTERS THE WAR ON THE SIDE OF THE ALLIES

15

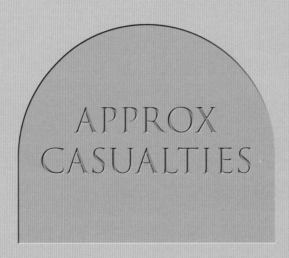

APPROX CASUALTIES

14TH OCT

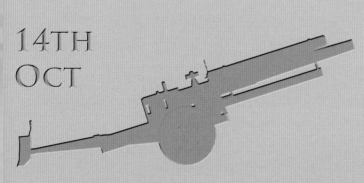

BULGARIA ENTERS THE WAR ON THE SIDE OF CENTRAL POWERS

ALLIED CASUALTIES
4,248,000

CENTRAL POWERS CASUALTIES
2,058,000

5TH JUNE

HMS *Hampshire* hits german mine. Lord Kitchener drowns

1ST JULY

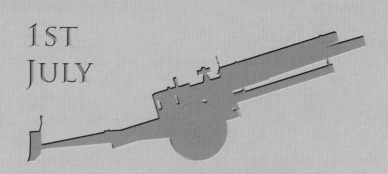

First day of the battle of the somme

4 MAIN BATTLES

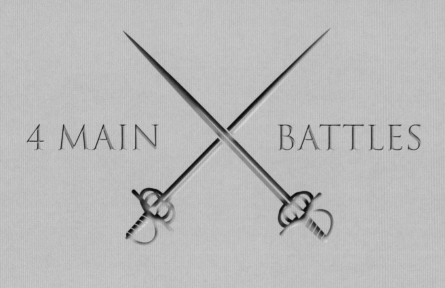

—— VERDUN ——
(21st February)

—— JUTLAND ——
(31st May)

—— BRUSILOV ——
(4th June)

—— SOMME ——
(1st July)

19

8TH OCT

German air force officially established

15TH SEP

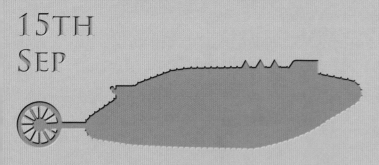

OPERATIONAL DEBUT OF THE TANK

17TH SEP

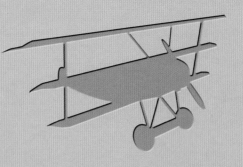

MANFRED VON RICHTHOFEN CLAIMS HIS FIRST 'KILL'

APPROX CASUALTIES

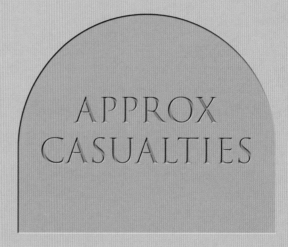

ALLIED CASUALTIES
4,748,000

CENTRAL POWERS CASUALTIES
2,443,000

12TH DEC

GERMANY MAKES PEACE PROPOSAL. IT IS REJECTED

16TH JAN

MANFRED VON RICHTHOFEN IS AWARDED POUR LE MÉRITE

19TH APRIL

LARGE-SCALE MUTINIES OCCUR WITHIN FRENCH ARMY

4 MAIN  BATTLES

19

— ARRAS —
(9TH APRIL)

— SECOND AISNE —
(16TH APRIL)

— THIRD YPRES —
(31ST JULY)

— CAMBRAI —
(20TH NOVEMBER)

6TH NOV

CANADIAN TROOPS CAPTURE VILLAGE OF PASSCHENDAELE

15TH DEC

RUSSIA NEGOTIATES PEACE ON THE EASTERN FRONT

6TH APRIL

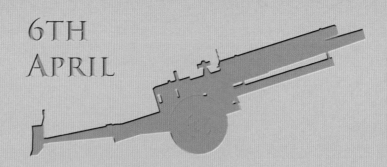

AMERICA DECLARES WAR ON GERMANY

17

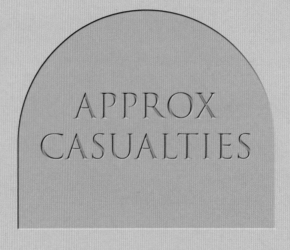

APPROX CASUALTIES

20TH NOV

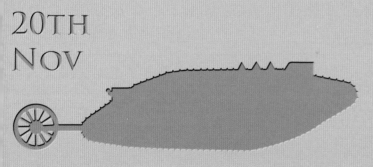

FIRST TANK LED OFFENSIVE LAUNCHED AT CAMBRAI

ALLIED CASUALTIES
3,371,502

CENTRAL POWERS CASUALTIES
1,278,220

21ST MAR

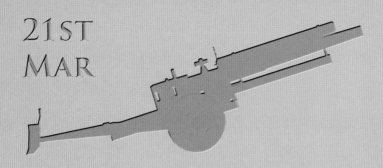

6,500 GERMAN GUNS FIRE OVER 1,100,000 SHELLS IN 5 HOURS

1ST APRIL

THE ROYAL AIR FORCE IS OFFICIALLY ESTABLISHED

19

4 MAIN BATTLES

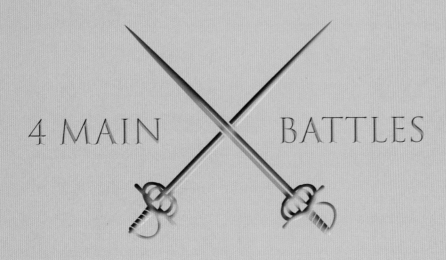

·SPRING OFFENSIVE·
(21ST March)

–SECOND MARNE–
(15TH July)

—AMIENS—
(8TH August)

2ND BATTLE of ALBERT
(21ST August)

4TH NOV

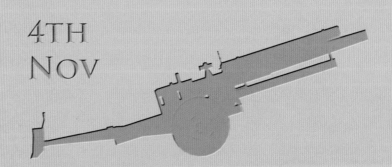

ATTACK ON THE SAMBRE CANAL – LAST BIG ALLIED OFFENSIVE

21ST APRIL

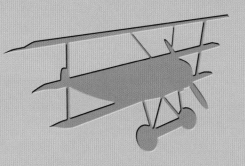

BARON VON RICHTHOFEN IS SHOT DOWN AND KILLED

28TH OCT

AUSTRIA OFFICIALLY ASKS FOR ARMISTICE

11TH NOV

GERMANY SIGNS THE ARMISTICE ENDING THE WAR

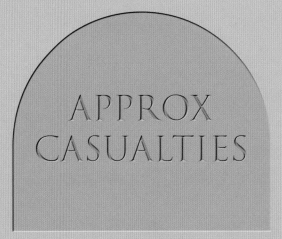

APPROX CASUALTIES

ALLIED CASUALTIES 2,620,000

CENTRAL POWERS CASUALTIES 2,750,000

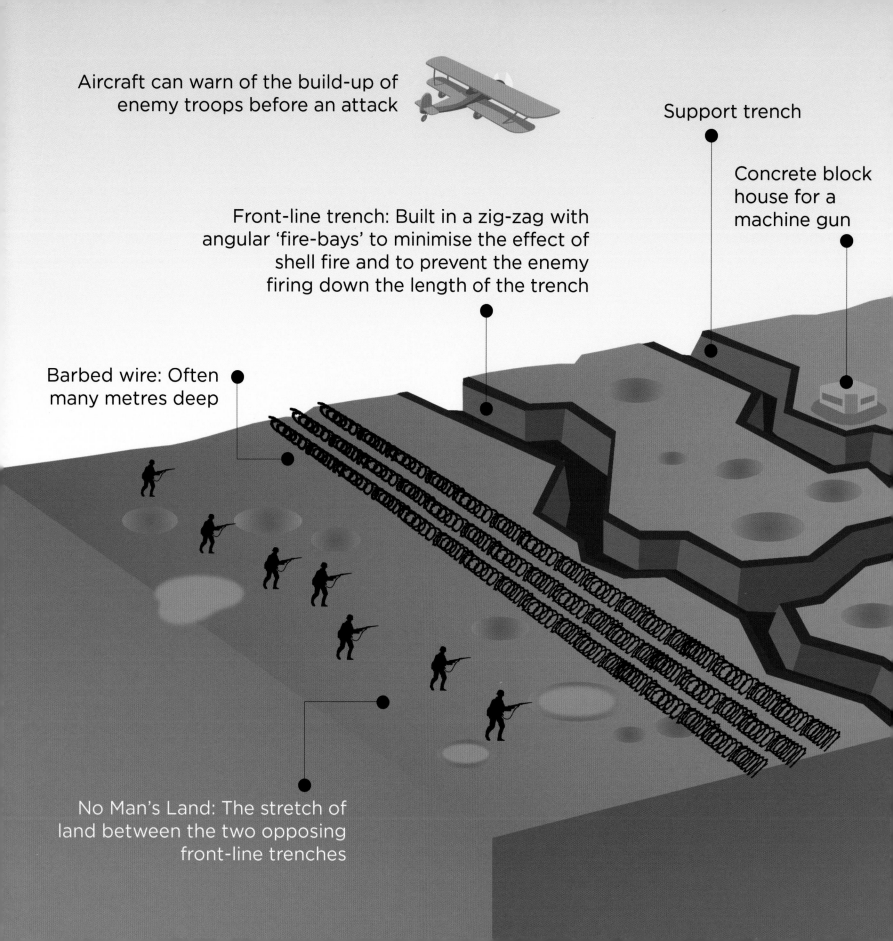

Aircraft can warn of the build-up of enemy troops before an attack

Support trench

Concrete block house for a machine gun

Front-line trench: Built in a zig-zag with angular 'fire-bays' to minimise the effect of shell fire and to prevent the enemy firing down the length of the trench

Barbed wire: Often many metres deep

No Man's Land: The stretch of land between the two opposing front-line trenches

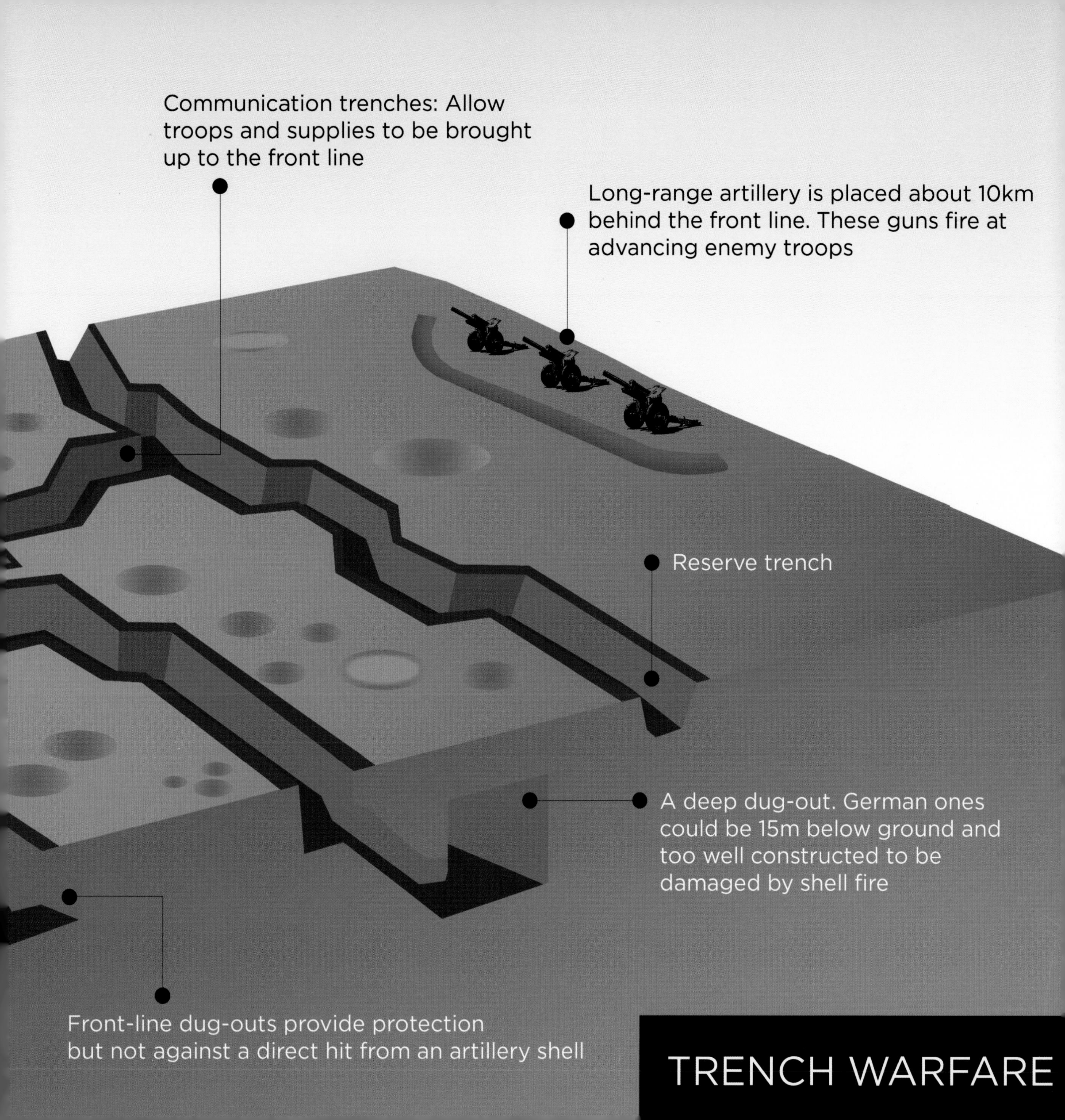

Communication trenches: Allow troops and supplies to be brought up to the front line

Long-range artillery is placed about 10km behind the front line. These guns fire at advancing enemy troops

Reserve trench

A deep dug-out. German ones could be 15m below ground and too well constructed to be damaged by shell fire

Front-line dug-outs provide protection but not against a direct hit from an artillery shell

TRENCH WARFARE

'FIRSTS'

THE FIRST WORLD WAR SAW NUMEROUS WAR 'FIRSTS' THROUGHOUT THE DURATION OF THE CONFLICT; LET'S LOOK AT SOME

FIRST TIME BRITAIN ENFORCED 'BLACKOUT' RESTRICTIONS

FIRST EVER AIR ASSAULT ON BRITAIN
(19 Jan 1915)

FIRST USE OF MASS AEROPLANE SQUADRONS
FOR STRATEGIC BOMBING
(France, Sep 1914)

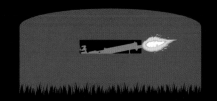

FIRST USE OF CONCRETE BUNKERS

FIRST TIME THAT BRITAIN AND THE US
FOUGHT TOGETHER AS ALLIES

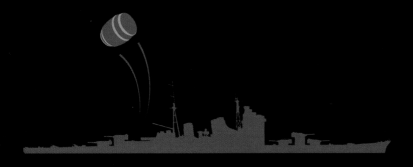

FIRST USE OF DEPTH CHARGES
(British Navy, 1915)

FIRST USE OF THE FLAME THROWER
(German Army, Oct 1914)

**FIRST WAR WHERE MORE SOLDIERS WERE
KILLED IN COMBAT THAN FROM DISEASE**

FIRST USE OF MUSTARD GAS
(German Army, Sep 1917)

FIRST USE OF PROPAGANDA WAR ART
(German Army, Oct 1914)

FIRST WAR IN WHICH COMBAT STRESS / PTS DISORDER WAS RECOGNISED AS A CONDITION

FIRST USE OF SUB-MACHINE GUNS

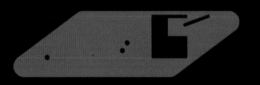

FIRST TANK TO BE USED IN BATTLE
(British Army, Sep 1916)

Number Of Men Mobilised

Mobilisation during the war by major combatants

Russia: 12,000,000 ·······································

Germany: 11,000,000 ·································

Britain: 8,905,000 ···································

France: 8,410,000 ·····························

Austria-Hungary: 7,800,000 ·············

Italy: 5,615,000 ·················

USA: 4,355,000 ·············

64.7 MILLION MEN MOBILISED IN TOTAL

FIGHTING MEN

After all the political showboating, feather ruffling and finger pointing, it was down to the ordinary soldier to fight it out in the trenches. The First World War was the first conflict that saw mass conscription from the ordinary civilian classes. Millions of men from all walks of life, such as teachers, bankers, plumbers, shopkeepers, farmers, labourers and office workers, were called up to serve with the forces and answer the call of their country.

THE
BRITISH SOLDIER
★ ★ ★ ★ ★ ★ ★ 1914-1918 ★ ★ ★ ★ ★ ★ ★

MINIMUM AGE
18
TO VOLUNTEER

15%
OF WARTIME VOLUNTEERS WERE UNDERAGE

OFFICER   TOMMY

5'5"
average height of a recruit

1 stone
average weight put on in a year

8 stone
average weight of a recruit

80lb
average kit weight of a recruit

30
average age of a recruit

BRITISH ARMY ORIGINS:

IRELAND
134,202 men

WALES & MONMOUTH
272,924 men

SCOTLAND
557,618 men

ENGLAND
4,006,158 men

DAILY SALARY (1914)

Private: 1s 0d

Sergeant: 2s 4d

Lieutenant: 8s 6d

Major: 16s 0d

Lt-Colonel: 28s 0d

1s is roughly equivalent to £3.14 in today's money

RATIONS (1914)

10oz of meat & 8oz of vegetables per day

The British Army employed 300,000 field workers to cook and supply food

PUNISHMENTS

Extra Fatigues
Not Saluting / Being Late

28 Days' Detention
Disobeying / Being Drunk

Put to Death
Desertion / Cowardice

FIGHTING EQUIPMENT

Rifle with Bayonet / Sling

Entrenching Tool

Rations and Water

Ammunition (270 rounds)

Plus accoutrements, such as belt, water bottle, etc. **Total Weight: 50–55lb**

THE
GERMAN SOLDIER
MORE COMMONLY KNOWN AS 'LANDSER'

20
THE AGE MOST GERMAN MEN STARTED THEIR SERVICE

OFFICER

PRIVATE

EACH YEAR BETWEEN
400,000 & 500,000
MEN BECAME ELIGIBLE

35%
OF GERMANS WERE REJECTED AS BEING UNFIT

EVERY
72
SECONDS A GERMAN SOLDIER DIED DURING THE WAR

The German Empire
The German soldiers of the First World War did not belong to a single army but to one of four armies representing the kingdoms of the German Empire

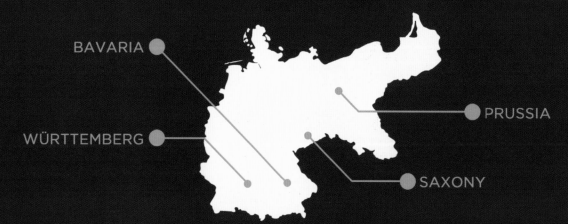

BAVARIA

PRUSSIA

WÜRTTEMBERG

SAXONY

DAILY SALARY (1914)

Soldat: 0.7 marks

Gefreiter: 0.75 marks

Unteroffizier: 1.6 marks

Sgt/Unteroffizier: 2.25 marks

Vizefeldwebel: 2.53 marks

Leutnant: 4.10 marks

Hauptmann: 9.33 marks

Oberst: 24 marks

RATIONS (1914)

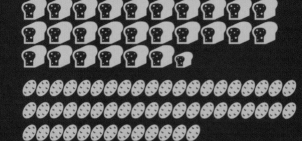

26.5oz of bread, 53oz of potatoes and 4.5oz of veg

INFANTRY RANKS

German Army	British Army
Musketier (Prussian)	Private
Infanterist (Bavarian)	Private
Soldat (Saxon)	Private
Gefreiter	Lance Corporal
Obergrefreiter	Senior Lance Corporal
Unteroffizier	Corporal
Feldwebel	Sergeant Major
Etatmassige Feldwebel	Staff Sergeant Major
Feldwebelleutnant	Second Lieutenant
Leutnant	Lieutenant
Hauptmann	Captain
Oberstleutnant	Lieutenant Colonel
Oberst	Colonel
Generalmajor	Brigadier General
Generalleutnant	Lieutenant General
General der Infanterie	Infantry General
Generalfeldmarschall	General Field Marshal

FIGHTING EQUIPMENT

The German infantry soldier wore the famous spiked helmet (*pickelhaube*) with front and rear visor, found to be inadequate and phased out from 1916

The helmet was covered with a grey cotton cover with the regimental number stencilled on in green

THE
AMERICAN SOLDIER
COMMONLY KNOWN AS 'DOUGHBOY'

126,000
THE SIZE OF THE US ARMY IN 1914

4,355,000
MEN WERE MOBILISED BY THE END OF THE WAR

200,000
THE NUMBER OF AFRICAN AMERICAN SOLDIERS WHO SERVED IN THE WAR

THEY WERE FORCED TO SERVE IN SEGREGATED UNITS

ONLY
11%
SAW FRONT LINE ACTION.
MOST SERVED IN LABOUR UNITS

US troops helped build up French infrastructure during 1917–18:

- 82 new ship berths

- 1,000 miles of railway track

- 100,000 miles of telephone and telegraph lines

FINAL CASUALTY

The last American soldier killed was Private Henry Gunther, who was killed at 10.59 on 11 November 1918. Officially, Gunther was the last man to die in WW1

His divisional record stated:

'Almost as he fell, the gunfire died away and an appalling silence prevailed'

RATIONS

16oz of hard bread

12oz of bacon

1.2oz of coffee

1.4oz of sugar and 0.16oz of salt

SOLDIERS' PAY

The monthly salary for each of the main ranks in the US Army:

Salaries from 1914

Private 1st Class
$30

Corporal 1st Class
$36

Sergeant 1st Class
$38

Battalion Sergeant Major
$48

Regimental Sergeant Major 1st Class
$51

HATS OFF!

The US soldier Montana hat

American soldiers were easily distinguished on the Western Front by their Montana hat. However, it offered no protection from bullets or the weather

400,000 British steel helmets were purchased until the US M1917 helmet was issued – it was practically identical to the British version. Some units also wore the French Adrian helmet

THE
AUSTRALIAN SOLDIER

★ ★ ★ KNOWN AS ANZACS/DIGGERS ★ ★ ★

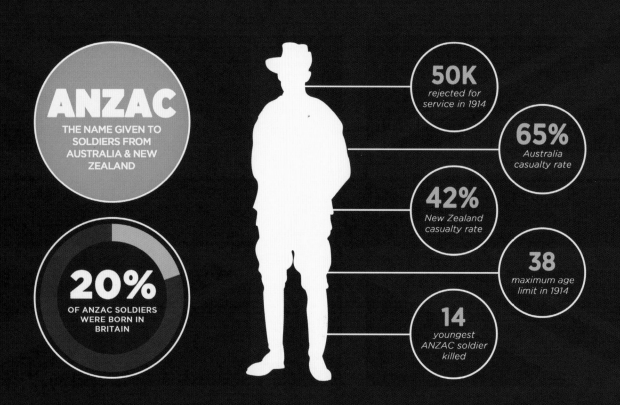

ANZAC
THE NAME GIVEN TO SOLDIERS FROM AUSTRALIA & NEW ZEALAND

20%
OF ANZAC SOLDIERS WERE BORN IN BRITAIN

50K
rejected for service in 1914

65%
Australia casualty rate

42%
New Zealand casualty rate

38
maximum age limit in 1914

14
youngest ANZAC soldier killed

416,809 Australians enlisted for service in the First World War:

Queensland
57,705 enlisted

Tasmania
15,485 enlisted

West Australia
32,231 enlisted

Victoria
112,399 enlisted

South Australia
34,959 enlisted

New South Wales
164,030 enlisted

ANZAC'S SET UP

38.7%
of Australian male population between 18 and 45 enlisted for service

42%
of New Zealand men of military age enlisted

VICTORIA CROSS

75 ANZAC soldiers were awarded the Victoria Cross during the war

SHRINKING DIGGERS

In 1914 the Australian army set a minimum height requirement of 5ft 6in. Preference was given to those men who had prior military experience

1914   1915

By July 1915 the minimum height requirement had fallen to 5ft 2in and the age limit had risen from 38 to 45 as new men were needed to replace Gallipoli casualties

DIGGER PAY

Australian troops were paid a minimum of 6 shillings a day which was more than 3 times the pay of the average British private

Six shillings per day was slightly under minimum wage in Australia but, due to unemployment and tough financial conditions, this kind of money was still attractive to many

THE
FRENCH SOLDIER
MORE COMMONLY KNOWN AS 'POILU'

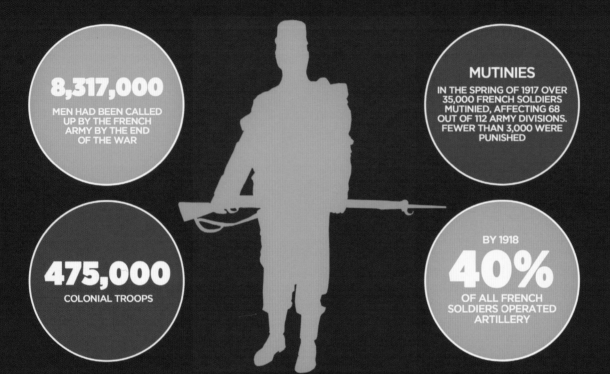

8,317,000
MEN HAD BEEN CALLED UP BY THE FRENCH ARMY BY THE END OF THE WAR

475,000
COLONIAL TROOPS

MUTINIES
IN THE SPRING OF 1917 OVER 35,000 FRENCH SOLDIERS MUTINIED, AFFECTING 68 OUT OF 112 ARMY DIVISIONS. FEWER THAN 3,000 WERE PUNISHED

BY 1918
40%
OF ALL FRENCH SOLDIERS OPERATED ARTILLERY

Weight of the average French soldier's pack
40KG(88lb)

French soldiers were generally expected to move almost everywhere on foot. They were also required to carry with them clothing, bedding, food and drink – including a wine ration – equipment and ammunition
The combined weight of the backpacks carrying all this usually exceeded 40kg (88lb)

Each soldier carried the *vivres des reserve* reserve ration in his pack. This consisted of: 2 tins of boiled beef or corned beef, 12 biscuits, 2 packets of dried soup, 2 coffee tablets and 2 issues of sugar

COMPULSORY
21
SERVICE AGE

75%
OF RUSSIAN ARMY WERE KILLED, CAPTURED OR WOUNDED

Papakha
the sheepskin hat made famous by the Russian Cossacks

1.42m
size of Russian army at the start of war

6.5m
size of Russian army at the end of 1914

18
no. of years of military service

75%
the illiteracy rate among Russian troops

The average Russian soldier exhibited the same characteristics as their ancestors – resolution, endurance and loyalty

However, they were often let down by inept leadership, poor supplies and inadequate levels of equipment

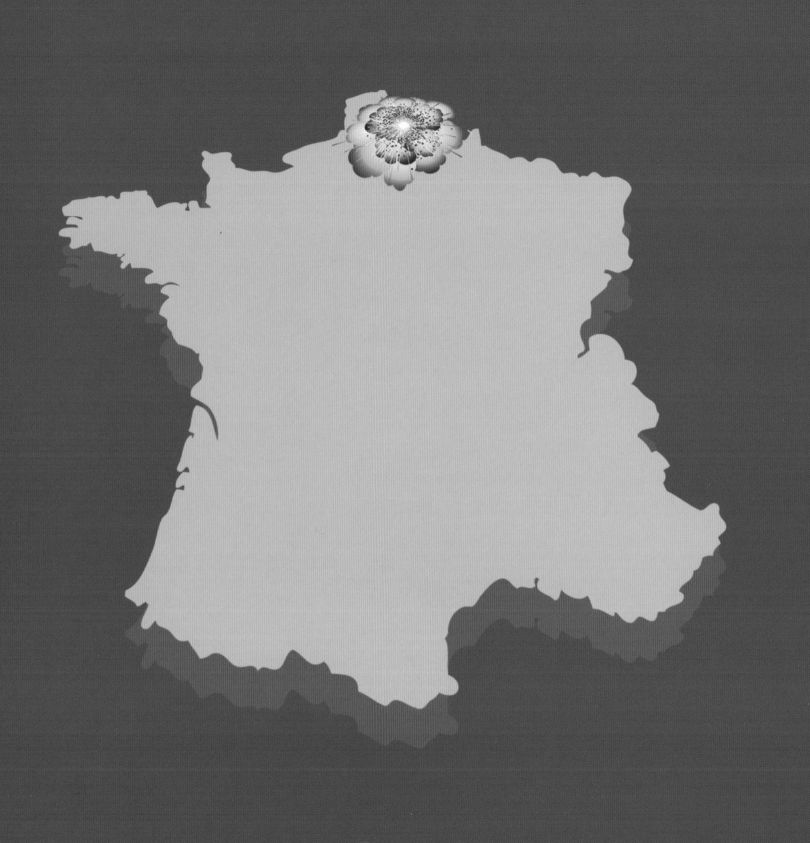

INFANTRY BATTLES

The soldiers who occupied the front-line trenches were in almost constant engagement, either directly or indirectly, with the enemy, even where there was no official offensive or 'big push' taking place. Trench raids, enemy snipers, poison gas, indiscriminate grenade and mortar fire, and of course enemy artillery meant that front-line troops were in persistent danger. If this wasn't enough, large-scale offensives unleashed firepower on an industrial scale. Many of these conflicts have gone down in history as some of the most destructive and costly battles of all time.

BATTLE *of* MONS

23 – 24 August 1914

Sir John French and Sir Horace Smith-Dorrien VS *Alexander von Kluck*

The first contact between the enemies was made on 21 August when a British bicycle reconnaissance team encountered a German unit near Obourg. Further to the rear, the rest of the BEF dug in along the Mons–Condé canal.

After a dawn artillery bombardment, the first waves of German infantry rushed the bridges on the canal at 9am. Despite facing hugely superior numbers, the British riflemen held their lines and inflicted heavy casualties.

By mid afternoon, the British were forced to retreat towards Maubeuge and on to Le Cateau almost 20 miles away. However the retreat would become more than ten times that distance.

Mons

BELGIUM

 The BEF were highly trained and during the battle maintained such a high rate of fire with their rifles that the German attackers were convinced they were facing machine guns

80,000
British Soldiers

300
British Guns

160,000
German Soldiers

600
German Guns

5,000
German losses during the battle were in excess of 5,000

1,638
The BEF suffered 1,638 casualties during the battle

Four Victoria Crosses won during the first day of fighting at Mons

250m
The furthest advance of any Allied force was 5 miles

Allenstein

POLAND

BATTLE *of* TANNENBERG

23 – 30 August 1914

General Paul
von
Rennenkampf
 vs
Paul von Hindenburg
and
Erich Ludendorff

The Battle of Tannenberg was the first major battle on the Eastern Front. Russia was advancing quickly through East Prussia, getting closer to Germany, which made the German high command very nervous.

Reinforcements were rushed in from the Western Front, and when Russian messages were intercepted the Germans knew that they had an opportunity for victory.

On 27 August the Germans attacked Samsonov's Second Army. The exhausted Russian troops were critically short of supplies. By the 29th they were completely surrounded and cut off. Of 150,000 men, only 10,000 escaped.

The Battle of Tannenberg actually took place close to Allenstein, 20 miles to the west. It was named Tannenberg afterwards to associate it with one of 1410 fought by German Teutonic Knights

Russian Losses:

50 THOUSAND
Casualties
(killed/missing/wounded)

500
Pieces of captured
artillery

92 THOUSAND
Prisoners
of war

60,000
The number of loaves of bread demanded by the Russian Army

10,000
Out of an estimated 150,000 men in the Russian Second Army, only 10,000 escaped

After the battle Samsonov committed suicide

Germany was forced to transfer 85,000 from the Western Front, adding to the failure to occupy Paris

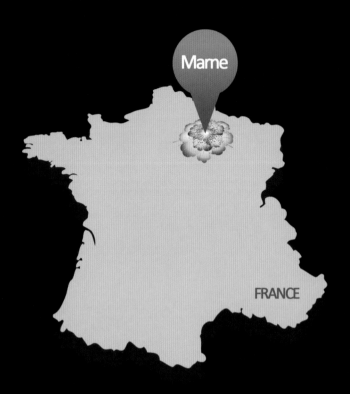

Marne

FRANCE

BATTLE *of the* MARNE

5–12 September 1914

Sir John French and
Commander in Chief
Joseph Joffre
 VS
Commander Karl
von Bulow and General
Alexander von Kluck

After the setback at Mons the German army regrouped and continued its march on Paris. After losing a small scuffle at Guide, von Kluck moved his army round which opened up a 30-mile gap between him and von Bulow.

French air reconnaissance noticed this and alerted the infantry to the possibility of a counter attack, which was launched on 6 September, achieving complete surprise.

The Germans had no choice but to withdraw to the north, destroying everything as they went in an effort to slow down the Allied pursuit.

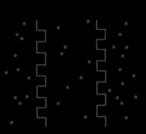

The Battle of the Marne signalled the end of the mobile war and the beginning of trench warfare that is so synonymous with the First World War.

250,000
French Casualties

220,000
German Casualties

80,000
British Casualties

2 mil
Over 2 million men fought in the Battle of the Marne

81,700
The number of Allied soldiers who died during the battle

600 Parisian taxi cabs were used to transport French reserves into battle

40m
The German retreat to the north covered 40 miles

Ypres

BELGIUM

FIRST BATTLE *of* YPRES

19 October – 22 November 1914

Sir John French, Albert I of Belgium, Marshal Ferdinand Foch VS *Generalfeldmarschall Albrechy, Duke of Württemberg, Rupprecht*

The battle began with a nine-day German offensive that threatened to cut clean through the Allied lines. The line held just long enough to allow the deliberate flooding of the battlefield, providing a 20-mile-long belt of marshland.

Ypres was not flooded though, and on 31 October the Germans attacked the town directly. It seemed inevitable that Ypres would fall – even the Kaiser arrived at the front to witness victor – but the line held. Just.

Fighting around Ypres continued until 22 November when the onset of winter forced a break in hostilities.

R.I.P
BEF

The fighting around Ypres in 1914 effectively destroyed the BEF as an effective fighting force

80,000
French Casualties

134,000
German Casualties

55,000
British Casualties

21,562
Belgian Casualties

During the battle, cooks, orderlies and support staff fought the German attackers

260,000

Total casualties on all sides (killed, missing and wounded) was over 260,000

The BEF hung on to Ypres partly due to its proficiency in rapid rifle fire

2:1

From mid-October the German Army had a numerical superiority of almost 2:1

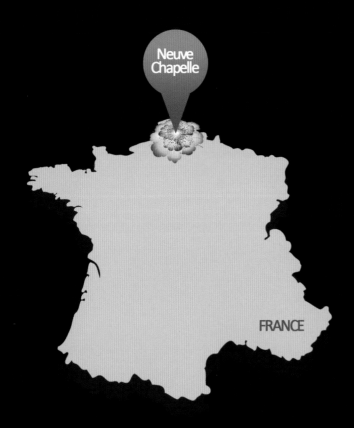

Neuve
Chapelle

FRANCE

BATTLE *of* NEUVE CHAPELLE

10 – 13 March 1915

Sir John French  VS *Crown Prince Rupprecht*

Although Neuve Chapelle was the initial target of the assault, the British intended to put on to the east towards Lille.

Initial progress was rapid, with British and Indian infantry quickly breaking through sections of the weakly held German line. Neuve Chapelle was secured in 4 hours, although supply and communication issues made further advance difficult.

A German counter attack was launched on 12 March and recovered some ground but the Allies held on. A further attack on Aubers ridge proved futile and the attack was called off.

The Battle of Neuve Chapelle was the first British-led offensive of the war, and saw several innovations such as in-depth air reconnaissance, precision time-tables for artillery, and a dedicated light railway to take supplies to the front

10,600
German Casualties

7,000
British Casualties

4,200
Indian Casualties

4 hrs
The time taken for the Allies to secure the village of Neuve Chapelle

10,000
The number of German soldiers involved in the counter attack of 12 March

The 35 minute artillery bombardment fired more shells than the South African war

2km
The amount of land re-captured by the Allies in the battle

GALLIPOLI

Gallipoli

TURKEY

18 March 1915 – 9 January 1916

Admiral Sir John
Michael de Robeck &
General Ian Standish
Monteith Hamilton

 VS

Mehmed Esad
Pasha & General
Leutnant Otto Liman
von Sanders

Originally a naval operation, the main reason to attack this
area was to open up more reliable supply routes with Russia,
via the Black Sea.

There was also a feeling among senior British leaders that, due to
a stalemate on the Western Front, a new front was needed to
ensure progress in the war.

Six VCs Before Breakfast

On the morning of 25 April 25 1915, 950 men of the
1st Battalion. Lancashire Fusiliers landed at 'W' beach.
By the time the beach was secured,
they had suffered 543 casualties.
Six Victoria Crosses were awarded that morning

140,887

Allied Casualties

250,000

Ottoman Empire
Casualties

6

There were 6 weeks between
the initial naval bombardment
and the infantry invasion

ANZAC

This was the first time ANZAC
(Australian & New Zealand troops)
went into action in the war

145,000

An estimated 145,000 British
soldiers suffered from dysentry
or diarrhoea

There are 31 Commonwealth
War Grave Cemeteries on the
Gallipoli peninsula

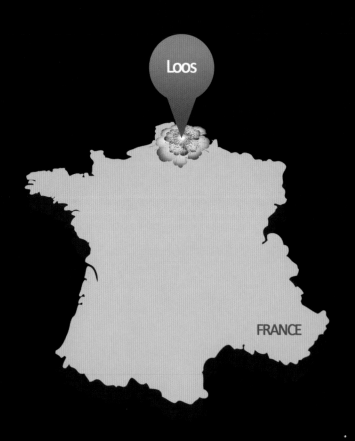

Loos

FRANCE

BATTLE *of* LOOS

25 September – 14 October 1915

Sir John French and Field Marshal Douglas Haig *vs* *Crown Prince Rupprecht*

The Battle of Loos was a joint Anglo-French offensive and at the time was the biggest battle the British Army had fought in its history. It was also the first time Kitchener's New Army was used in battle.

Haig was not happy with the terrain his army had to advance over, plus he had a severe shortage of trained men, guns and shells.

Despite the British using gas for the first time, the results of the offensive were mixed. The town of Loos was captured but consolidation proved impossible and the attack came to a halt at Hill 70.

The Battle of Loos saw the British use gas for the first time in warfare. 5,100 cylinders of chlorine gas were released towards the German lines before the first attack

72,000
British Casualties

25,000
German Casualties

2,880

The number of British officers that became casualties during the battle

5,100

The number of gas cylinders released towards the German lines on 25 September

250,000 artillery shells were fired in the four-day preliminary bombardment

The British suffered 2,632 casualties from their own gas attack

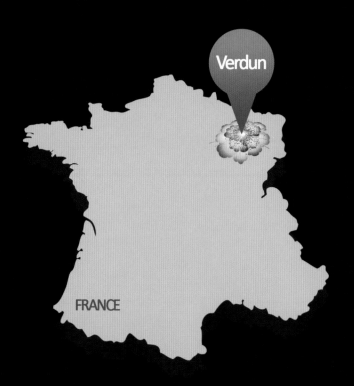

Verdun

FRANCE

BATTLE *of* VERDUN

21 February 1916 — 18 December 1916

 VS

General
Philippe Pétain

General
Erich von Falkenhayn

An attritional battle, instigated by Germany to destroy the French army.

Falkenhayn chose Verdun because it had huge patriotic significance to the French, who would defend it to the last man.

377,000

French Casualties

Killed or missing: 162,000
✛ Wounded: 215,000

337,000

German Casualties

Killed or missing: 100,000
Wounded: 237,000 ✛

TOTAL FORCES ENGAGED

70%

25%

of the total French
Army fought at Verdun

of the total German
Army fought at Verdun

On the opening day of the battle, 1,220 German artillery pieces fired over 1 million shells on Verdun and the surrounding areas in a 9 hour period

300

The Battle of Verdun was not short, lasting for a massive 300 days

With the Battle of Verdun General Falkenhayn wanted to 'Bleed France White'

2.5km

On 23 July 23, the German Army got within 2.5km of Verdun

70%

At least 70% of all casualties in the Battle of Verdun resulted from artillery fire

BRUSILOV OFFENSIVE

4 June – 20 September 1916

UKRAINE

General Aleksei Brusilov VS *Count Franz Conrad von Hotzendorf and Alexander von Linsingen*

The offensive was launched to help relieve the pressure on France at Verdun and took place along a 200-mile front in modern-day Ukraine.

Initially the offensive was a success with the Austrians in full retreat, but a mixture of tired troops, overstretched supply lines and German reinforcements meant progress slowed and finally stopped in September.

With over a million casualties on either side, this was a very costly battle. As a result, Germany had been forced to move significant men and resources away from Verdun and the Austrian-Hungarian Army was practically destroyed.

With an estimated total casualty list of over 2.5 million men, the Brusilov Offensive was one of the most deadly battles in world history

Austro-Hungarian losses during the battle:

1 MILLION
Casualties
(killed/missing/wounded)

400 THOUSAND
Men taken
prisoner

25 THOUSAND
Square kilometres
of territory

75 miles
During the battle the Russians pushed some areas of the front line back up to 75 miles

100m
In many places the Russians crept up to within 100m of the Austrian lines to start the attack

2,000 Russian artillery guns were used in the preliminary bombardment

26,000
Approximate number of Austrian prisoners taken on the first day of the battle

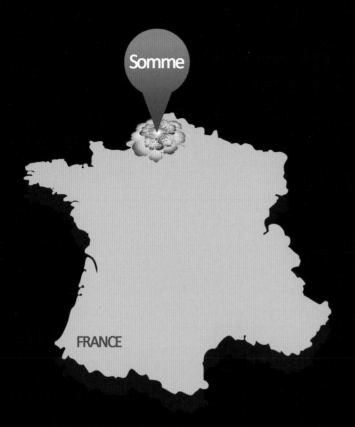

Somme

FRANCE

BATTLE *of the* SOMME

1 July 1916 – 18 November 1916

Field Marshal Douglas Haig & General Ferdinand Foch vs *General Max von Gallwitz & General Fritz von Below*

Originally planned as a French offensive with minimal British support, intended to smash the German Army and deplete its manpower.

With the German attack at Verdun, the French instead asked Britain to carry out a large diversionary attack to relieve pressure on the French Army.

The Battle of the Somme was one of the largest battles of the First World War; by the time fighting had petered out in late autumn 1916 the forces involved had suffered more than 1 million casualties, making it one of the bloodiest military operations ever recorded.

 On the first day of the battle, the British Army suffered 57,470 casualties and it stands out as the darkest moment in the army's history.

419,654
British Casualties

204,253
French Casualties

500,000
German Casualties
(approx figure)

8 days
The initial pre-battle artillery bombardment lasted 8 days

19,240
19,240 British soldiers died on the first day of the battle

The British used tanks for the first time in battle on 15 September 1916

5 miles
The furthest advance of any Allied force was 5 miles

Ypres

BELGIUM

3RD BATTLE *of* YPRES

PASSCHENDAELE

31 July 1917 – 10 November 1917

General Sir
Herbert Plumer &
General Sir
Hubert Gough

 VS

Crown Prince
Rupprecht & General
Eric Friedrich
Wilhelm Ludendorff

Haig was convinced the fighting of 1916 (Somme and Verdun) had weakened the German Army and wanted to deliver the knockout blow in Flanders.

As well as being Haig's preferred region for a large attack, the Royal Navy were worried about intense German submarine activity emanating from the Belgian ports and implored Haig to capture these areas.

The Ypres offensive of 1917 was severely hampered by the heaviest rain in 30 years, which churned the Flanders lowland soil into a thick muddy swamp. The movement of troops, supplies and guns was severely disrupted.

250,000

Allied Casualties

260,000

German Casualties

4,000

On the first day, British forces of XVIII and XIX Corps advanced 4,000 yards

5

In just over 100 days of fighting, the Allies managed to advance a little over 5 miles

3,000

3,000 guns of various shapes and sizes were used in the offensive at Ypres

4.25m

In the 10-day preliminary bombardment, 4.25 million shells were fired by the Allies

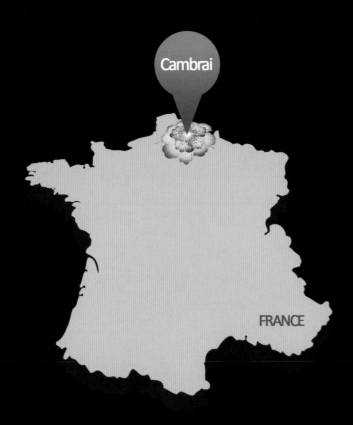

Cambrai

FRANCE

BATTLE *of* CAMBRAI

20 November – 8 December 1917

General
Julian Byng  VS General Georg von
der Marwitz

After the disaster of Passchendaele, Haig was keen to finish 1917
on a positive note and turned to the Tanks Corps to help him
break the Hindenburg Line.

Over 300 tanks were used in the initial assault, and by the end of the
first day the Hindenburg Line had been broken, with advances of
several miles in some areas.

179 tanks were lost on that first day and the momentum
quickly dwindled. Within 1 week the Germans had recaptured most of their
early losses.

TANK LOSSES ON THE FIRST DAY

65

DESTROYED BY
THE ENEMY

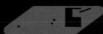

43

DITCHED

71

MECHANICAL
FAILURE

The Battle of Cambrai was the first
battle in history in which tanks were
used in large numbers to spearhead
an offensive

90,000

Approximate number of
total casualties suffered by
both sides during the battle

1,003

The number of British
artillery guns used as
the battle began

The success of the first day
resulted in the ringing of church
bells across Britain

5 miles

Advances of up to 5 miles
in some areas were achieved
on the first day

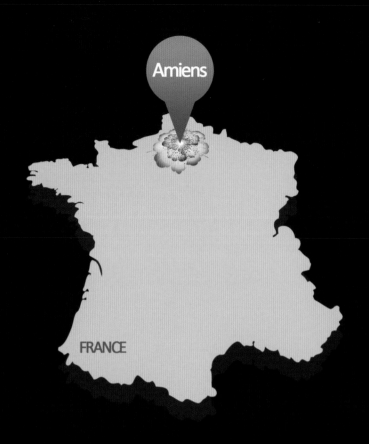

Amiens

FRANCE

KAISERSCHLACHT
THE GERMAN SPRING OFFENSIVE OF 1918

21 March 1918 – 12 June 1918

Haig, Foch,
Pétain, Pershing
and Tarnagnini
de Abreu

 VS

Erich
Friedrich
Wilhelm
Ludendorff

Germany knew that their only chance of winning the war was to knock out the Allies before the extra resources of men and material from the USA could be deployed. The main thrust of the attack was against the British towards the town of Amiens. It was thought that after the British were defeated the French would quickly look for peace.

Amiens was a strategically important supply town with a large railway hub that supported both British and French armies. If this town was captured it would severely impede Allied supply.

Operation Michael

There were four separate German attacks, codenamed *Michael, Georgette, Blücher-Yorck* and *Gneisenau*, and launched in that order. *Michael* was the main attack. The main aim of the first attack was to cut through the Somme, cut off British communications and move north west, surrounding the BEF in a small area of Flanders

539,739
Allied Casualties

519,000
German Casualties
(approx figure)

1.1m
The opening barrage fired 1.1 million shells on the British lines in 5 hours

21,000
During the first day 21,000 British soldiers were taken prisoner

German long-range guns were now able to fire on Paris. 183 huge shells landed on the city

After initial success, the Kaiser decorated Hindenburg with the Iron Cross with Golden Rays

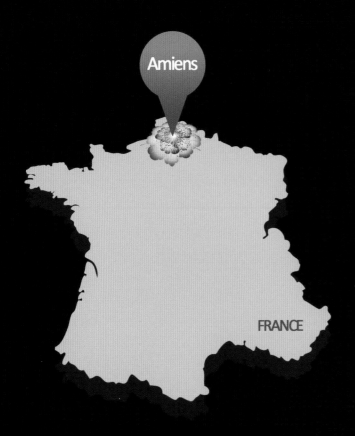

Amiens

FRANCE

BATTLE *of* AMIENS

8–12 August 1918

General Ferdinand Foch, Sir Henry Rawlinson, Sir John Monash, Sir Arthur Currie, General John Pershin VS *General Georg von der Marwitz & General Erich Ludendorff*

After the German offensives of 1918 Foch wanted to flatten out some salients along the line, including one at Amiens. So on 8 August thousands of Allied soldiers, backed by 500 tanks, attacked that area.

By early afternoon Canadian and Australian troops in the centre of the front had advanced 7 miles. Overstretched communication and supply lines caused the offensive to lose momentum quickly . By 11 August there were only a few tanks left working.

After the battle fighting continued in the area, eventually forcing the Germans to retreat to the Hindenburg Line.

8th AUGUST 1918: A BLACK DAY FOR GERMANY

30,000
German Casualties

20,000
German Prisoners

Such huge losses led Ludendorff to remark that the first day of the battle was 'the black day of the German Army'

100 DAYS

This battle heralded the start of the Allied Hundred Days Offensive which resulted in the final defeat of Germany and the end of the war

6

The number of operational tanks left by the 11th August

24

By the end of the day a gap of 24km (15 miles) had been punched in the German lines south of the Somme

Over 1,900 Allied planes were used in the attack

22,000

Approximate Allied casualties for the battle (killed/missing/wounded)

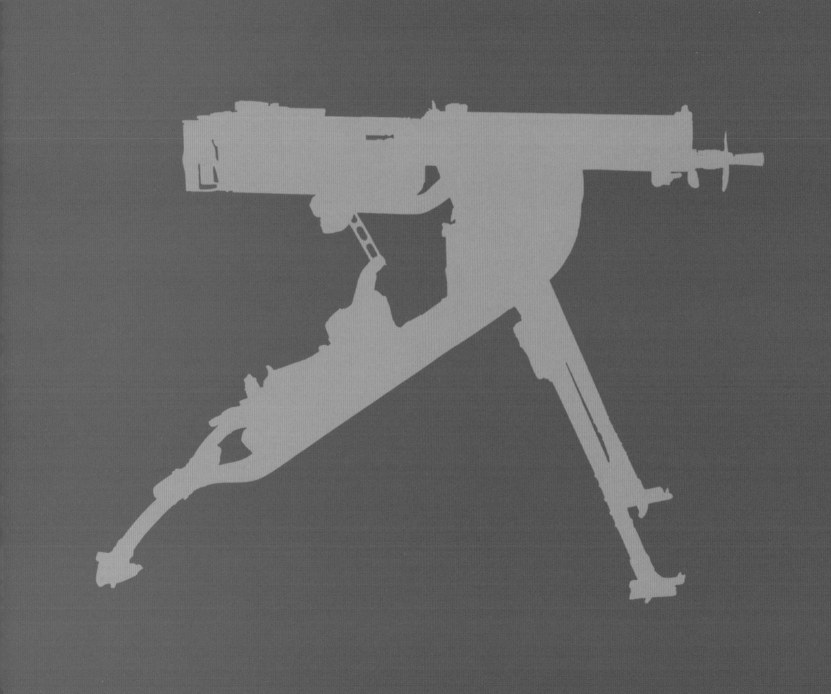

WEAPONS

The First World War was a war of invention. The science of killing advanced so quickly that the weapons and tactics evident up and down the lines in 1918 were unrecognisable from those that the first soldiers who went to war in 1914 had at their disposal. New weapons such as poison gas and tanks were inventions born out of the First World War, whereas more traditional firepower such as artillery and the machine gun benefitted from significant technological and tactical improvements that made them much more effective killing machines than they were before.

The Rifle

(first appeared in 1824)

German Mauser Gewehr 98 (G98) Rifle

 THE PROS

- The number one infantry weapon of the war, due to its light weight, accuracy and dependability
- In the hands of properly trained soldiers, this was a formidable and accurate weapon

👎 THE CONS

- The German Mauser rifle in 1914 had a magazine that could hold only five bullets
- Although it was extremely accurate, the rifle lacked the destructive firepower of mortars or machine guns

DID YOU KNOW? During the Battle of Mons in 1914, the small but highly trained BEF fended off a much larger German force with fire from their Short Magazine Lee–Enfield (SMLE) rifles. Their fire was so intense, Germans were convinced they were facing machine guns.

British Short Magazine 'Lee-Enfield'

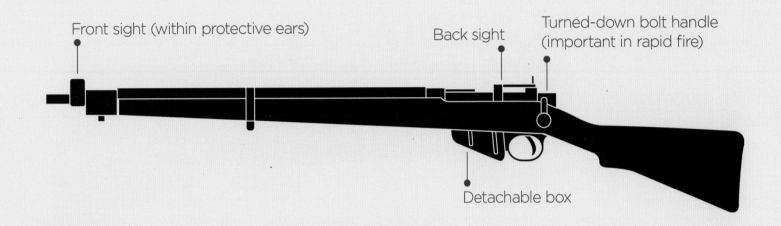

Front sight (within protective ears)

Back sight

Turned-down bolt handle
(important in rapid fire)

Detachable box

Calibre: .303 inch
Overall length: 44.5 inches
Barrel length: 25.19 inches
Magazine (full): 10 rounds
Weight: 8.12lb
Muzzle velocity: 2,060ft/sec

First produced in 1907
Designed by an American called James Lee and built at the Royal Small
Arms Factory in Enfield – hence the rifle's name
A well-trained infantryman could expect to fire 12 rounds a minute
The Lee-Enfield had one major weakness: the firing mechanism was
susceptible to failure due to dirt and grit. Keeping the rifle clean, especially in
the muddy trenches, was vitally important

Canadian 'Ross' Mark III B

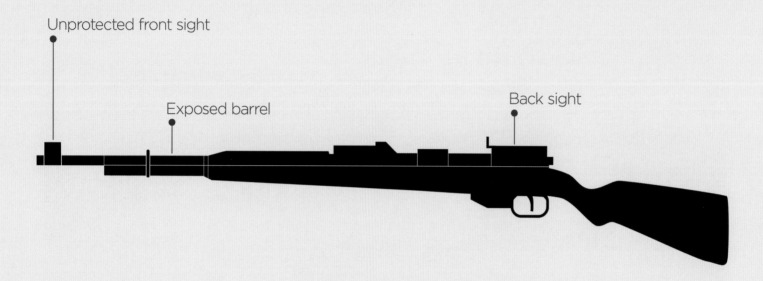

Unprotected front sight

Exposed barrel

Back sight

Calibre: .303 inch
Overall length: 50.5 inches
Barrel length: 30.5 inches
Magazine (full): 5 rounds
Weight: 9.75lb
Muzzle velocity: 2,060ft/sec

First developed in 1903
Named after its developer: Sir Charles Ross
A superbly crafted weapon superior to the British Lee–Enfield in both range and accuracy. It was a favourite among Allied snipers
Not built to survive life in the trenches. It jammed easily in the muddy conditions and would often seize up during intense periods of rapid fire
By 1916 Canadian infantry were re-supplied with Lee–Enfield rifles, with the Ross relegated to being used for training purposes only

French 'Lebel' (Model 1916)

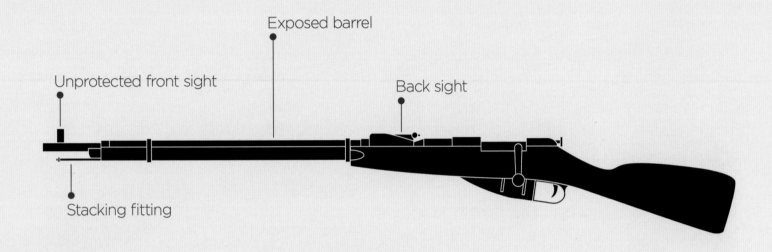

Exposed barrel

Unprotected front sight

Back sight

Stacking fitting

Calibre: 8mm
Overall length: 51.3 inches
Barrel length: 31.4 inches
Magazine (full): 8 rounds
Weight: 9.35lb
Muzzle velocity: 2,380ft/sec

First entered service in 1897
Effective range: 400m
Maximum range: 1,800m
The first military firearm to use smokeless gunpowder
A sturdy and reliable weapon
Poor sights hindered long-range use and the tube magazine was slow
and awkward to reload

German 'Mauser' (Model 1898)

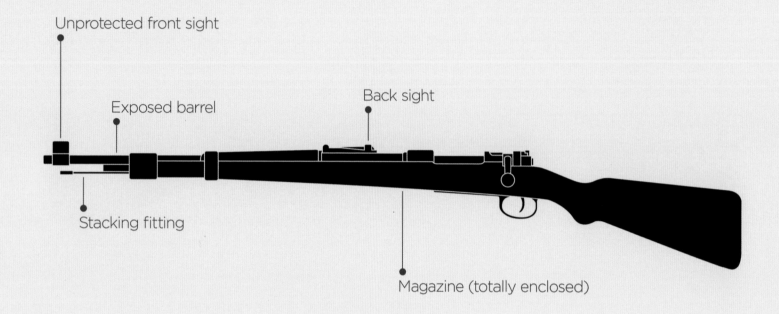

Unprotected front sight

Exposed barrel

Back sight

Stacking fitting

Magazine (totally enclosed)

Calibre: 8mm
Overall length: 49.25 inches
Barrel length: 29.15 inches
Magazine (full): 5 rounds
Weight: 9.5lb
Muzzle velocity: 2,500ft/sec

Patented by Paul Mauser on 9 September 1895
First use in combat during the Boxer Rebellion (1898–1901)
Metal parts of the rifle were prone to corrosion if not treated correctly
Effective range: 500m (800m with optics)

Italian 'Mannlicher-Carcano'

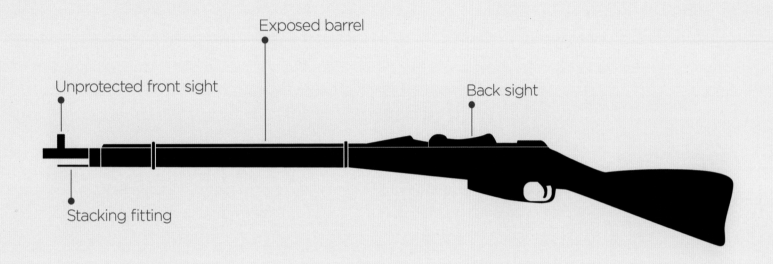

Exposed barrel

Unprotected front sight

Back sight

Stacking fitting

Calibre: 6.5mm
Overall length: 50.75 inches
Barrel length: 30.7 inches
Magazine (full): 6 rounds
Weight: 9lb
Muzzle velocity: 2,200ft/sec

Developed by Salvatore Carcano in 1890
Introduced in 1891
Effective range: 600m

Russian 'Moisin-Nagant'

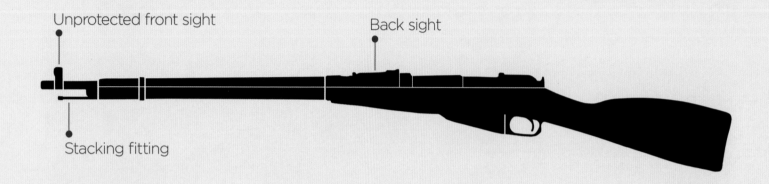

Unprotected front sight

Back sight

Stacking fitting

Calibre: 7.62mm
Overall length: 51.37 inches
Barrel length: 31.6 inches
Magazine (full): 5 rounds
Weight: 9.62lb
Muzzle velocity: 2,660ft/sec

Designed by Captain Sergei Mosin and Leon Nagant
Production commenced in 1892
Effective range: 500m (800m with optics)
By 1965, 37 million rifles had been produced

United States 'Springfield' (Model 1903)

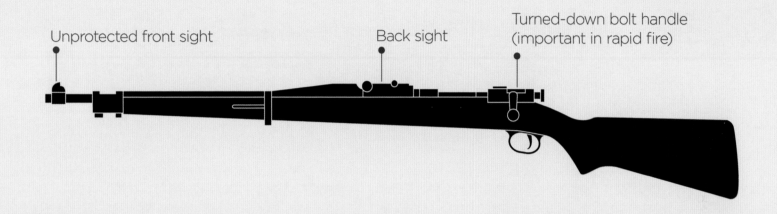

Unprotected front sight

Back sight

Turned-down bolt handle
(important in rapid fire)

Calibre: .03 inch
Overall length: 43.25 inches
Barrel length: 24 inches
Magazine (full): 5 rounds
Weight: 8.69lb
Muzzle velocity: 2,500ft/sec

By the time the US Army entered the First World War 843,239 rifles
had been produced
Several soldiers suffered severe injury due to brittle receivers
Effective range: 600m
A well-trained infantryman could achieve 15 rounds a minute
Remained in service throughout the Second World War, the Korean War
and the early stages of Vietnam

Pistols

(first recorded use in 1364)

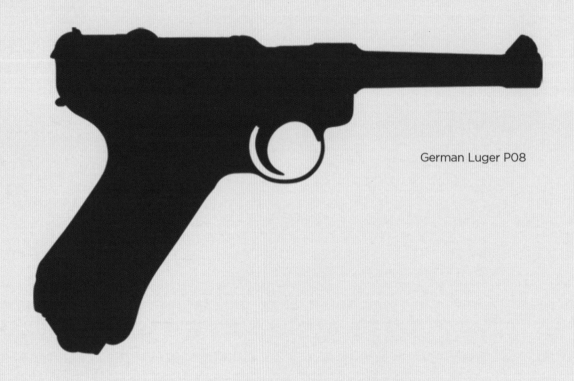

German Luger P08

👍 THE PROS

• Issued mainly to the officer class, they were useful in the tight confines of a trench
• Also used extensively by tank crews, miners, aircrew and other specialist roles where a rifle was simply too big

👎 THE CONS

• Pistols lacked the range and accuracy of a good rifle
• Because a pistol often identified an officer it made them easier for enemy snipers and gunners to identify and target

DID YOU KNOW?

One particular blowback pistol, the Belgian-made 7.6mm Browning Model 1900 played perhaps the most crucial part of the whole war, as it was this weapon that was used to assassinate Archduke Franz Ferdinand on 28 June 1914.

Colt M1911 Pistol

Country of origin: USA
First issued: 1911
Calibre: 11.43mm (0.45in)
Magazine: 7 rounds
Overall length: 210mm
Weight: 1.105kg (39oz)
Muzzle velocity: 251m/sec

After successful trials in which sample pistols fired 6,000 rounds over 2 days, the Colt M1911 Pistol was accepted by the US Army on 29 March 1911. It was accepted as standard issue in the Navy and Marine Corps in 1913

This semi-automatic, magazine-fed pistol was the standard-issue firearm for both world wars, the Korean War and Vietnam

Glisenti Model 1910

Country of origin: Italy
First issued: 1910
Calibre: 9mm (0.354in)
Magazine: 7 rounds
Overall length: 207mm
Weight: 0.82kg (29oz)
Muzzle velocity: 305m/sec

The Glisenti Model 1910 was a 9mm calibre semi-automatic service pistol produced by the Italian company Societa Siderugica Glisenti. It was put in production in 1910 to replace the ageing Bodeo Model 1889

Despite having a complex and weak firing system it saw extensive service in both world wars with the Italian Army

Luger P08

Country of origin: Germany
First issued: 1900
Calibre: 9mm (0.354in)
Magazine: 7 rounds
Overall length: 222mm
Weight: 0.87kg (31oz)
Muzzle velocity: 350m/sec

The Luger P08 (Pistole 08) was one of the first semi-automatic hand weapons and was first adopted by the Swiss Army in 1900

The Luger has a distinctive shape and is synonymous with the German Army of both world wars

Mauser C96 Automatic

Country of origin: Germany
First issued: 1894
Calibre: 7.63mm (0.3in)
Magazine: 10 rounds
Overall length: 280mm
Weight: 1.13kg (40oz)
Muzzle velocity: 440m/sec

Arguably the most powerful pistol in service during the war. First used by Turkish and Italian forces, the Imperial German Army ordered 150,000 Mauser C96 pistols modified to use a 9mm round due to shortage of the standard-issue Luger P08 pistol

They were nicknamed 'Red 9' because a large number 9 was painted in red on the grip handles to remind users of the correct type of ammunition

Modèle 1892 Revolver

Country of origin: France
First issued: 1893
Calibre: 8mm (0.314in)
Magazine: 6 rounds
Overall length: 240mm
Weight: 0.85kg (29.98oz)
Muzzle velocity: 220m/sec

Produced by Manufacture d'armes de Saint-Étienne, the Modèle 1892 revolver was the standard-issue sidearm in the French military during the First World War. It was well built and finished to a high standard

It fired single rounds by either cocking the hammer or via full pull of the trigger. Its major weakness was its lack of power

Steyr M1912

Country of origin: Austria
First issued: 1911
Calibre: 9mm (0.354in)
Magazine: 8 rounds
Overall length: 216mm
Weight: 1.02kg (36oz)
Muzzle velocity: 361m/sec

The Austrian-built Steyr M1912 pistol was a successful semi-automatic weapon that remained in service until after the Second World War. It was a good-quality weapon and was able to endure the tough conditions of trench warfare without much trouble

As a consequence it was a popular weapon that had a good reputation for consistent performance and durability

Webley Mark VI

Country of origin: Britain
First issued: 1913
Calibre: 11.4mm (0.455in)
Magazine: 6 rounds
Overall length: 235mm
Weight: 1.0kg (35oz)
Muzzle velocity: 190m/sec

At the outbreak of war the standard-issue revolver for the British and Commonwealth Armies was the Webley Mark V; however, by May 1915 this was replaced by the Mark VI which remained the standard weapon for the rest of the war

Issued to officers, airmen, naval crews, trench raiders, machine-gun teams and tank crews, it proved to be a reliable and well-regarded weapon. Tens of thousands were produced for the war

Machine Gun

(first appeared in 1884)

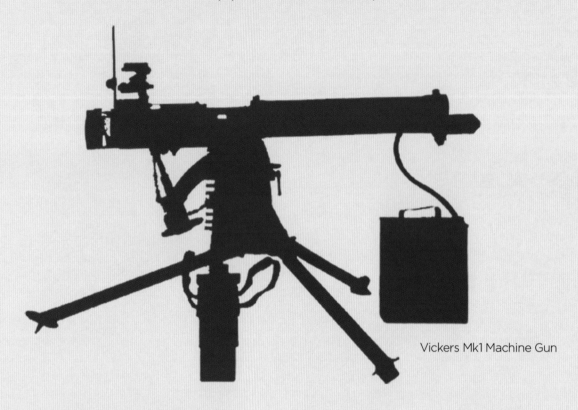

Vickers Mk1 Machine Gun

👍 THE PROS

- Fearsome defensive weapons when deployed correctly, they could dominate the battlefield
- One WW1 machine gun could match the power of around 80 rifles
- Also used effectively by tanks and the RAF

👎 THE CONS

- Limited attacking capability due to being very large and heavy (30 – 60kg)
- Needed up to 6 men to keep the gun firing
- Water-cooled variants often overheated and were prone to jamming

DID YOU KNOW?

The British did not create their Machine Gun Corps until October 1915. During the British attack at High Wood on 24 August 1916 it is estimated that 10 British Vickers machine guns fired over 1 million rounds in 12 hours.

Maschinengewehr 08 (German)

In service from: 1908
Weight: 56kg
Crew: 4-man crew
Cartridge: 7.92mm
Rate of fire: 450–500
rounds per minute
Max range: 3,500m
Muzzle velocity: 823m/sec

A very potent weapon, the Maschinengewehr 08 was the mainstay of the German Army's machine-gun units
The barrel was cooled by means of a water blanket wrapped around it which held 7.5 pints of water. The water would reach boiling point after 1 minute of continuous firing

Vickers Machine Gun (British)

In service from: 1912
Weight: 33kg
Crew: 3-man crew
Cartridge: 303 inch
Rate of fire: 450–500 rounds per minute
Max range: 4,500m
Muzzle velocity: 682m/sec

The Vickers was based on the 1884 Maxim automatic machine gun. It was lighter than the original Maxim and was a reliable weapon
They were still heavy and cumbersome to move around the battlefield, each belt of ammunition (250 rounds – about 30 seconds of continuous firing) weighed 10kg

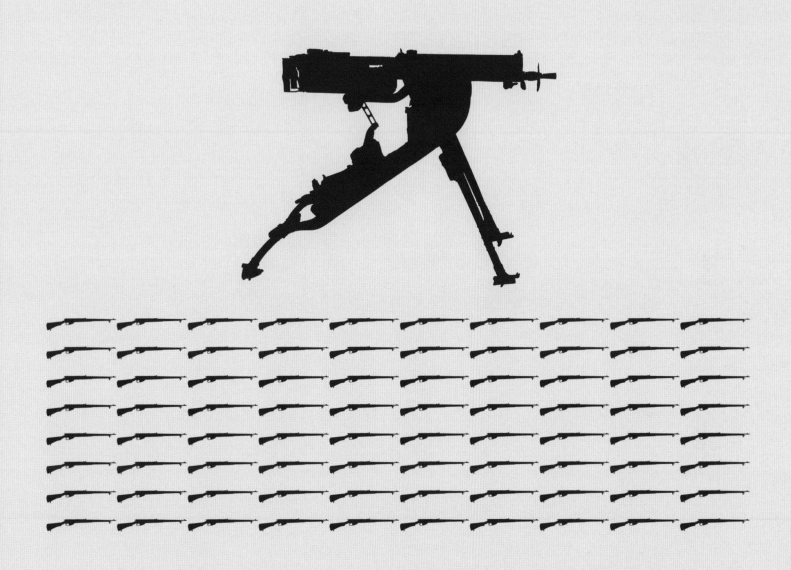

In 1914 the German high command calculated that the firepower of one heavy machine gun was equal to that of 80 riflemen

90%
British casualties

It is thought that 90% of all British casualties on the first day of the Battle of the Somme were caused by German machine guns

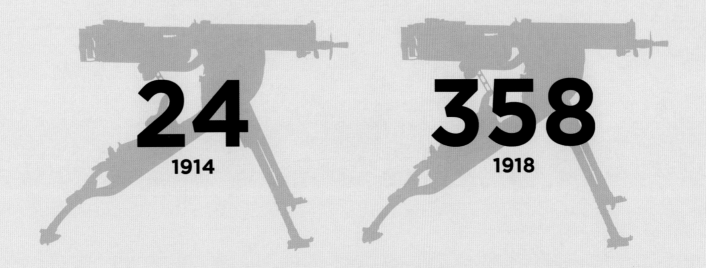

24 1914

358 1918

In 1914 the German army deployed an average of 24 machine guns per division. By early 1918 this had grown to 358

600
rounds per minute

Machine guns boasted impressive firepower – up to
600 rounds per minute

The average machine gun needed two or three men to
operate it, but often required a team of six men to manage it properly

65KG

The Maschinegewehr 08 (MG08) German heavy machine gun
weighed 65KG with tripod

Poison Gas

(first appeared in 1914)

WW1 Box Respirator

👍 THE PROS

- Had a huge psychological effect on soliders who were terrified of being gassed
- Wearing gas masks made firing weapons and communicating much more difficult
- Hugely debilitating when used in battle

👎 THE CONS

- Early tactics were dependent on wind to blow clouds of gas over the enemy; a shift in wind could be deadly to the attackers too
- After the initial panic and surprise had gone, gas accounted for relatively few battlefield deaths

DID YOU KNOW?

The first poison gas attack was by the Germans in 1915, using chlorine gas against French and Algerian troops. To counter the effects of poison gas, soliders were told to urinate on cloths and hold them to their face.

7.5% killed by gas

Only 7.5% of all men who were gassed were killed as a result

30

Approximately 30 different poisonous gases were used
during the First World War

1915
April 22nd

On 22 April 1915 Germany used clouds of chlorine gas for the first time as part of an infantry advance. The results were good. The assaulting troops advanced more than a mile within an hour, with hardly a shot fired

The French were the first to use gas in combat, using tear gas grenades against the Germans in August 1914

The first gas masks were nothing more than a pair of goggles and a piece of chemical-soaked cloth, but as war progressed gas protection became more sophisticated, culminating in full face mask and respirator

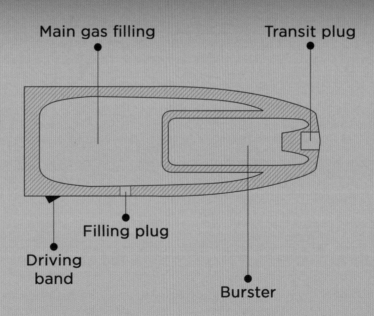

Gas was released in two different ways. Either by large canisters that released large quantities of gas vapour in the general direction of the enemy, or artillery shells were filled with liquid gas that evaporated when the shell burst

British and French
51,000 tons

Germans
68,000 tons

During the First World War, the Germans released about 68,000 tons
of gas, and the British and French released 51,000 tons

Grenades

(first appeared 15th Century)

WW1 Mills Grenade and German Stick Grenade

👍 THE PROS

- Perfect for clearing enemy trenches, dug-outs and pill boxes
- As they were relatively small, grenades could be carried by individual soldiers to complement their rifle

👎 THE CONS

- Early grenades in WW1 were prone to explode prematurely, making them very dangerous
- There were a large numqber of dud grenades, especially in the early part of the war

DID YOU KNOW?

On the night of 26 July 1916, at Poziers, British and Australian troops exchanged grenade fire with the enemy continuously for over 12 hours, throwing over 15,000 hand grenades.

German Stick Grenade

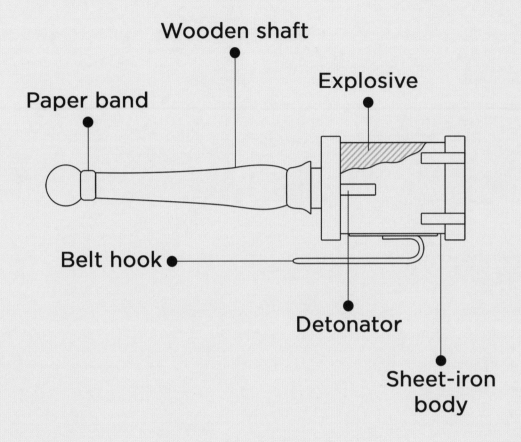

Paper band

Wooden shaft

Explosive

Belt hook

Detonator

Sheet-iron body

Officially known as the Model 24 Stielhandgranate. It was originally introduced in 1915 and the design was continually enhanced throughout the war

A pull cord ran down the hollow handle from the detonator within the explosive head, to a porcelain ball held in place by a detachable base closing cap. To use the grenade, the base cap was unscrewed, allowing the ball and cord to fall out. Pulling the cord dragged a roughened steel rod through the igniter causing it to flare-up and start the 5-second fuse burning

British 'Jam Tin' Bomb

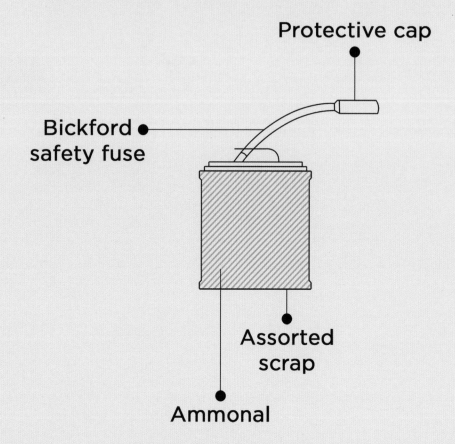

Protective cap

Bickford
safety fuse

Assorted
scrap

Ammonal

Officially known as the Double Cylinder No.8 (Light) and No.9 (Heavy) Hand Grenades, these early grenades were introduced in early 1915. A simple design made up of an inner can of explosive with an outer can of metal fragments or ball bearings. Due to huge demand, soldiers were forced to improvise and make their own crude versions of this grenade using a ration tin filled with explosive gun cotton and shrapnel balls

Jam Tin grenades were also used as booby traps – rigging the Jam Tin to a pressure trigger and leaving it under a heavy object to keep it unarmed

British Mills Hand Grenade

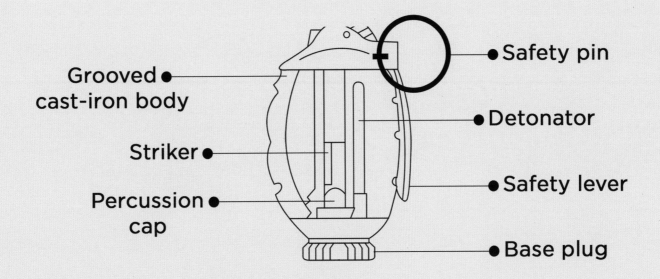

Grooved cast-iron body

Striker

Percussion cap

Safety pin

Detonator

Safety lever

Base plug

Introduced in May 1915. Named after its inventor, William Mills, although officially designated the 'Number 5 Grenade'. These grenades were very popular among the front-line troops – mainly due to their ignition system, which was activated when a ring was pulled and a lever released. Once released, the 4-second fuse gave the bomber time to throw the grenade

The body of the grenade was made from cast iron and weighed 1¼lb and was divided into sections to aid fragmentation and maximise damage

Throughout the war the design and components of the grenade were continually improved. It's estimated that over 70 million Mills grenades were thrown by the Allies during the war

British Newton Pippin Rifle Grenade

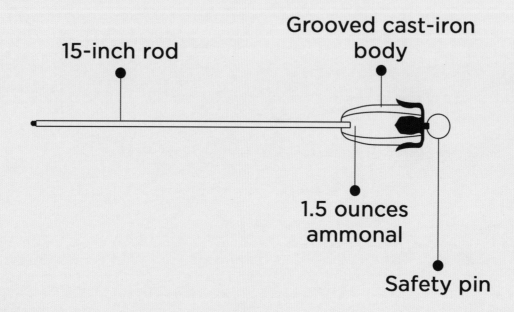

15-inch rod

Grooved cast-iron body

1.5 ounces ammonal

Safety pin

Introduced in June 1915. Named after its inventor, a British officer, Captain Henry Newton, although it was officially known as the 'Type 22 Rifle Grenade'. This started life as a simple percussion and time fuse hand grenade; Newton added a 15-inch rod and changed the shape to incorporate a sprung flat metal plate at the head as a detonation trigger

Range was around 300 yards. When the grenade hit a detonator would instantaneously explode the charge (ammonal or amatol). Because it was fired 'live' it was very dangerous and prone to exploding without notice

British 2-inch Trench Mortar 'Toffee Apple'

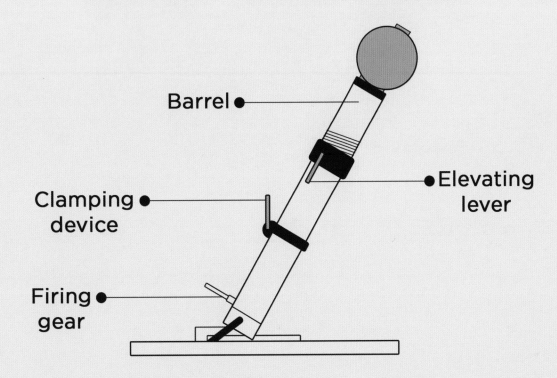

Barrel

Clamping device

Firing gear

Elevating lever

Officially known as the 2 inch Trench Mortar or 2 inch Howitzer, the Toffee Apple was used in significant numbers right up to 1918 when it was officially replaced with the Newton 6 inch mortar. One of the big advantages of the toffee apple was that it had a good blast effect and left no crater that could inconvenience advancing troops. Its intended role was to clear enemy wire and to damage enemy front line trench fortifications.

The ball part was roughly the size of a football, and was either filled with Amatol (identified by a painted green band) or Ammonal (painted pink band) attached to the end of a pipe, hence the nickname.

Knuckleduster Knife

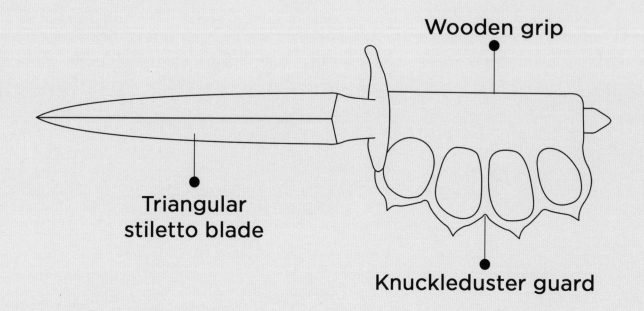

Wooden grip

Triangular
stiletto blade

Knuckleduster guard

The first official US trench knife adopted for service issue was the US M1917 trench knife designed by Henry Disston & Sons, and based on examples of trench knives used by the French Army. The M1917 featured a triangular stiletto blade, wooden grip, metal knuckle guard and a rounded pommel. The M1917 proved unsatisfactory in service, and a slightly improved version, the M1918, was adopted within months. The M1918 is almost identical to the M1917, differing primarily in the construction and appearance of the knuckle guard. Usable only as stabbing weapons, the M1917 and M1918 frequently suffered broken blades

Old Welsh Knife

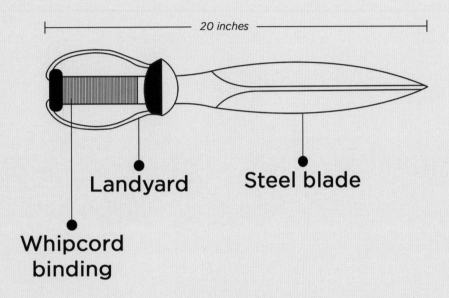

20 inches

Whipcord
binding

Landyard

Steel blade

Designed and manufactured by Joubert. This huge weapon was allegedly based on an ancient Welsh sword – the Cledd. It was 2ft long, had a 17.5-inch elliptical blade, and was 3 inches wide at broadest

The total number of knives manufactured is unknown; they were mainly issued to machine-gunners and bombers from trench stores as required. It was not available as general issue

Artillery

(first appeared in China during 12th Century)

British 18 Pounder Artillery Gun

👍 THE PROS

- With the onset of static trench warfare, artillery was the main weapon to smash trenches
- Technological advancement throughout the war led to increases in the rate of fire and improved accuracy of the guns

👎 THE CONS

- The very big guns were quite easy to spot from the air and had to move constantly
- The use of massed bombardments before large offensives gave the enemy plenty of warning of the impending attack

DID YOU KNOW?

WW1 artillery could be split into two distinct groups: field artillery and heavy artillery. Field artillery consisted of lighter, horse-drawn guns that were relatively quick to set up and break down. Heavier guns were much bigger and harder to move around.

Krupp 420mm Heavy Howitzer
'Big Bertha'

Capable of firing a 2,050lb (930kg) shell a distance of 9.3 miles (15km). It took a crew of 200 men 6 hours or more to assemble

Germany had 13 of these huge guns

British 18 Pounder Gun

The standard British field gun of the war. It was produced in large numbers and was even used for anti-aircraft work. Over 86 million British 18lb artillery shells were fired during the war – 52% of all shells fired by the Royal Field Artillery

The Paris Gun

The 'Paris Gun' was a German long-range
siege gun built by the German manufacturer
Krupp. Nicknamed the 'Paris Gun', it was the largest
piece of artillery used during the war and could fire a
210lb shell over 80 miles

It was developed as a psychological weapon to attack the
morale of the Parisians. When the first shell landed on Paris
on 21 March the public thought they were being bombed
by a high-altitude Zeppelin as the sound of neither a gun nor a
plane could be heard

367 shells fell on Paris in total, killing 256 civilians and wounding
another 620

A WEAPON LIKE NO OTHER

The paris gun was able to fire
a 100kg shell on to targets up to
81 miles away. Once fired the shell would
climb to an altitude of over 25 miles.
At the time it was the highest
altitude ever reached by a manmade
object. Each shell could travel
at over 3,600mph

A crew of 80
worked each gun
from the forest of
Courcey, 75 miles
NE of Paris

7 barrels were
constructed but
none were
captured

1,600

The number of artillery pieces that were involved in the British preliminary bombardment that preceded the Battle of the Somme

32,000,000

During the Battle of Verdun it is estimated that over 32 million artillery shells were fired

Canon de 75 modèle 1897 – the 'Soixainte-Quinze'

This French field gun was one of the most famous guns of the war. A superb weapon with a fast rate of fire (up to 30 rounds per minute in extreme circumstances) and a range of 9,000 yards

3,000

The Allies used over 3,000 artillery guns of various shapes and sizes during the Third Battle of Ypres

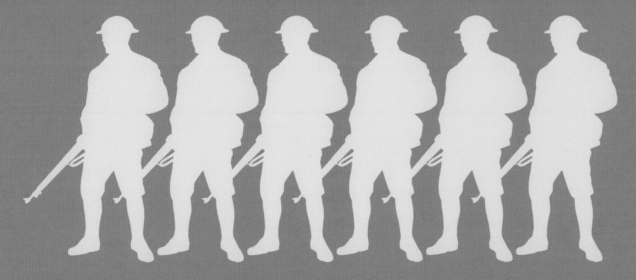

A typical field artillery piece required a team of 6: an NCO in command who received and gave orders; a layer who was responsible for the alignment and elevation of the gun; a gunner who worked the breech; and 3 men for handling the shells and fuses

Tank

(first appeared 15th September 1916)

British MKI

👍 THE PROS

- Tanks were able to cross any terrain, including trench systems
- In November 1917, a massed tank attack in Cambrai managed to advance four miles and break the Hindenburg Line

👎 THE CONS

- Early designs had almost zero visibility and were very slow
- The crew sat right next to the engine and as a result they were often poisoned by fumes

DID YOU KNOW?

British tanks were initially called landships. However, in an attempt to disguise them as water storage tanks rather than weapons, they were code-named 'tanks'. The name stuck

Genesis

A Landship Committee was established on 20 February 1915 by Winston Churchill (the First Lord of the Admiralty) to deal with the design and construction of what would turn out to be tanks

The name 'tank' has its origin within the code name for 'mother' which was 'Water Carrier for Mesopotamia'. This soon became shortened by the factory workers to 'tank', a nickname which quickly became officially adopted

1915
LITTLE WILLIE

The first completed prototype was running by December 1915; it was nicknamed Little Willie. However, a new improved design was already under construction, known as either Big Willie, Her Majesty's Land Ship Centipede or Mother. This new design made Little Willie redundant

The name Little Willie is said to be an uncomplimentary dig at the German Crown Prince

The first 50 tanks arrived in France on 30 August 1916 and were added to the Machine Gun Corps

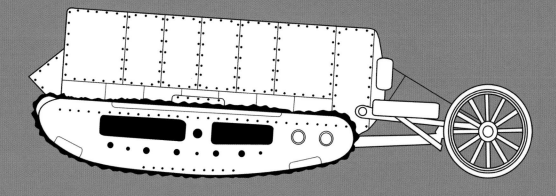

MKI Tank

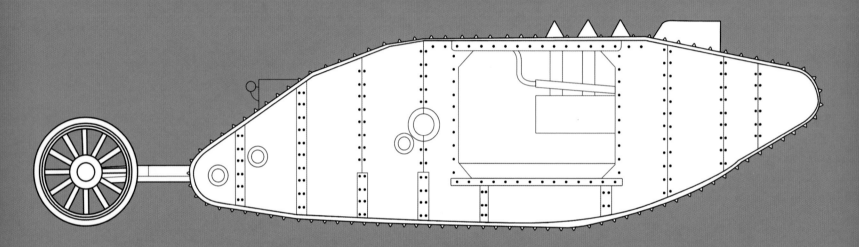

The first ever combat tank was the Mark I. It was first used in action during the morning of 15 September 1916 during the Battle of Flers-Courcelette

MKI Tank

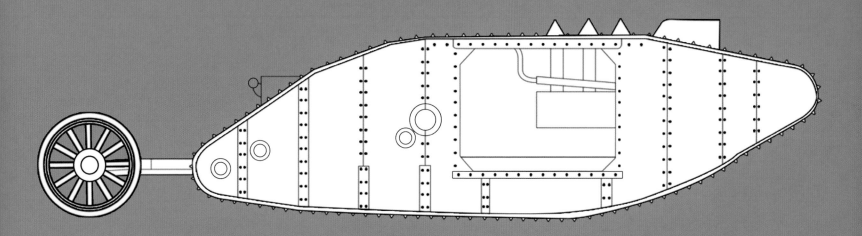

Country of origin: Great Britain
Number built: 150 (75 male and 75 female)
Year: 1916
Crew: 8
Speed: 4.5km/h
Armour: 6–12mm
Range: 37km
Firepower (male): 2 x 6 pounder guns and 3 x 8mm Hotchkiss machine guns
Firepower (female): 4 x .303 Vickers machine guns and 1 x 8mm Hotchkiss machine guns

Schneider CA1 Tank

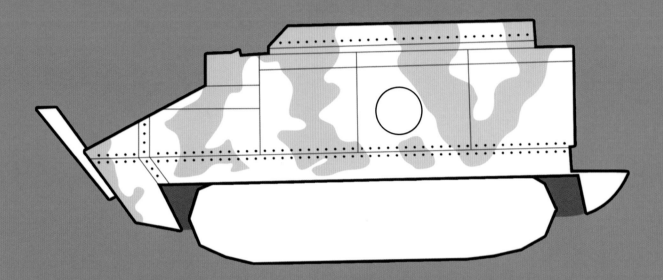

Country of origin: France
Number built: 400
Year: 1916/17
Combat debut: Berry-au-Bac, 16 April 1917
Crew: 6
Speed: 8km/h
Armour: 5–11mm
Range: 48–75km
Firepower: 75mm Blockhaus Schneider and 2 x 8mm Hotchkiss
machine guns

MKV Tank

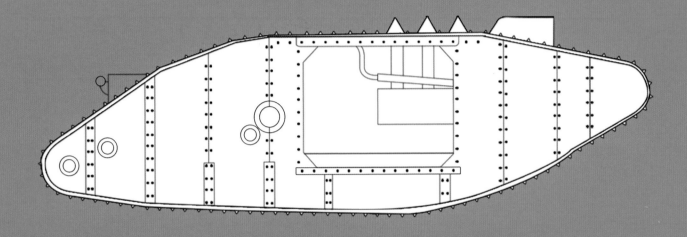

Country Of Origin: Great Britain
Number Built: 400 (200 male and 200 female)
Year: 1917
Combat Debut: Battle of Hamel, 4th July 1918
Crew: 8
Speed: 7.5km/h
Armour: 8-16mm
Range: 72km
Firepower (male): 2 x 6 pounder guns and 4 x .303 Hotchkiss machine guns
Firepower (female): 6 x .303 Hotchkiss machine guns

Renault FT Tank

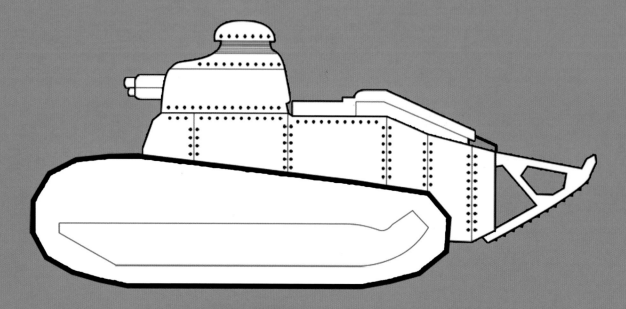

Country of origin: France
Number built: 3177
Year: 1917/18
Combat debut: Ploisy-Chazelle, 31 May 1918
Crew: 2
Speed: 7km/h
Armour: 30mm
Range: 65km
Firepower: Puteaux SA 1918 37mm gun or 8mm Hotchkiss
machine gun

A7V Tank

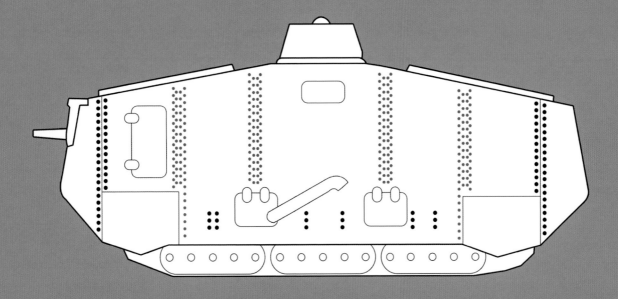

Country of origin: Germany
Number built: 20
Year: 1918
Combat debut: 21 March 1918
Crew: 18
Speed: 15km/h
Armour: 20–30mm
Range: 30–80km
Firepower: 1 x 57mm gun and 6 x 7.9mm machine guns

MK A Whippet Tank

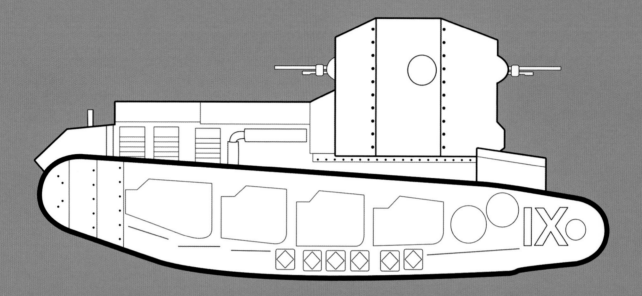

Country of origin: Great Britain
Number built: 200
Year: 1918
Combat debut: March 1918
Crew: 3
Speed: 13km/h
Armour: 5–14mm
Range: 64km
Firepower: 4 x .303 Hotchkiss machine guns

MKV* Tank

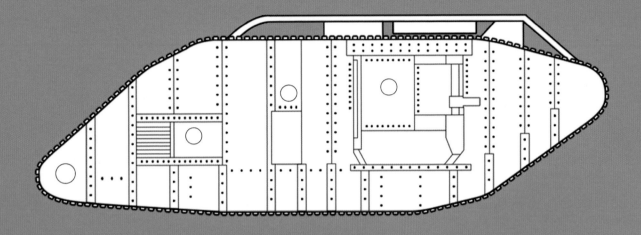

Country of origin: Great Britain
Number built: 579
Year: 1918
Combat debut: Battle of Amiens, August 1918
Crew: 8
Speed: 8km/h
Armour: 8–16mm
Range: 72km
Firepower (male): 2 x 6 pounder guns and 4 x .303 Hotchkiss machine guns
Firepower (female): 6 x .303 Hotchkiss machine guns

The British MKV* (pronounced Mark Five Star) Tank carried an extension of the tracks (called an unditching beam or a tadpole tail) to help it cross the wide trenches of the Hindenburg Line

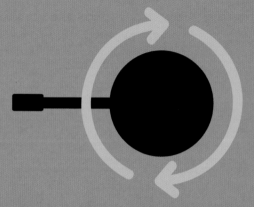

The French-built Renault FT was the first tank to have its main gun housed within a turret that could rotate 360 degrees

50°C

In early British tanks the engine was in the same place that the crew worked. Temperatures inside reached 50 degrees Celsius

Early tanks had no wireless radio, so communication with command posts was made by pigeons

The number of German tanks – the A7V – that saw combat in the First World War

With poor ventilation, British tank crews were often poisoned by engine and gun fumes

Early British Tanks had 2 variations, male and female, the difference being that the female was equipped with only machine guns whilst the male also had 6 pounder guns

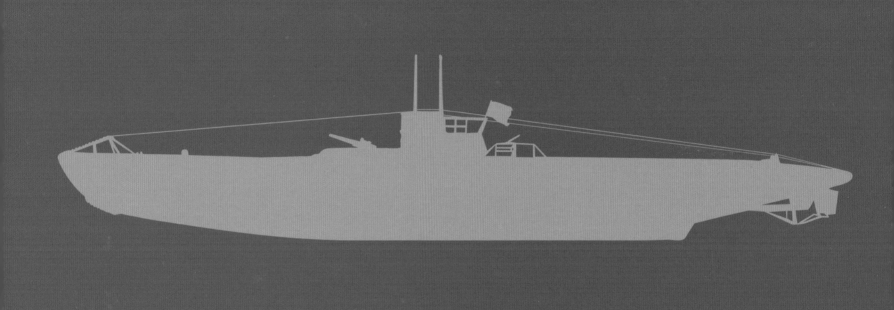

THE WAR AT SEA

The naval war, although perhaps not as dramatic or explosive as the air or land wars, had huge repercussions that were felt throughout all other theatres and aspects of the conflict. Germany's submarine warfare tactics, which included laying hundreds of mines across busy shipping lanes and conducting intermittent unrestricted submarine warfare, killed the British Minister for War, Lord Kitchener, influenced infantry tactics and decision making, and can be seen to be the *casus belli* for the USA to enter the war. Add to this the naval blockade of Germany and the decisive role the Merchant Navy had in supplying Britain and the Allies with materials and resources, and it is easy to see how important this aspect of the war really was.

Allied Naval Strength, August 1914

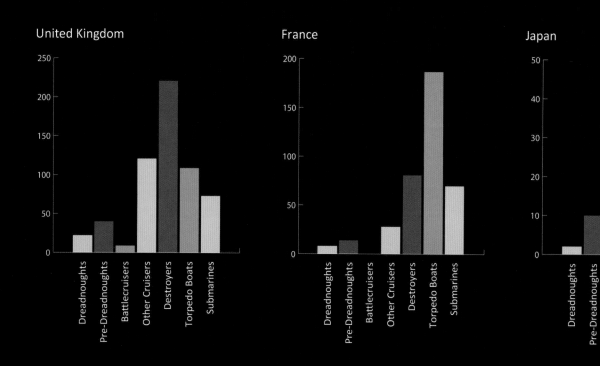

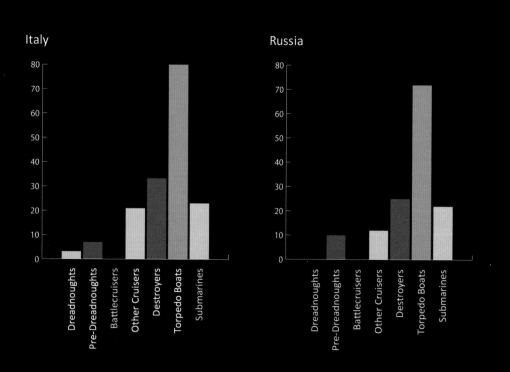

Central Powers Naval Strength, August 1914

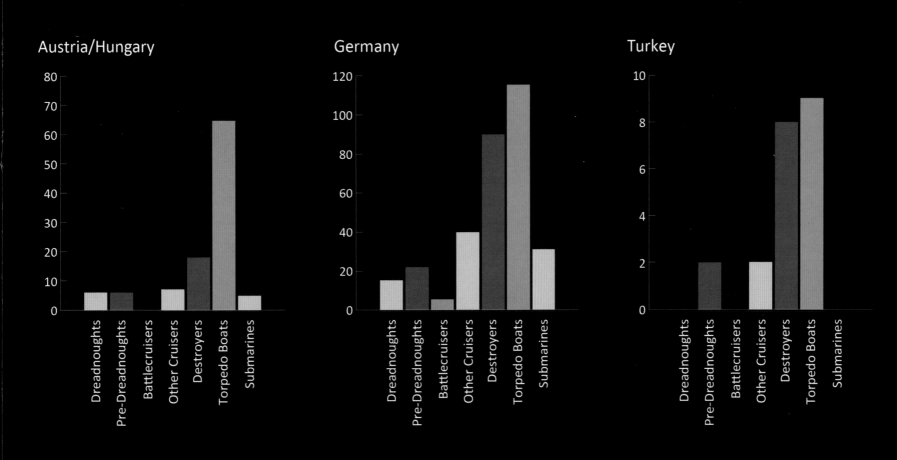

During the First World War the Royal Navy lost:

2 dreadnoughts

3 battlecruisers

11 battleships

25 cruisers

54 submarines

64 destroyers

10 torpedo boats

Aboukir   *Cressy*   *Hogue*

On 22 September 1914 German U-boats sunk 3 British ships (*Aboukir, Cressy* and *Hogue*) with the loss of 1,400 sailors

A total of 16,500 depth charges were expended by Britain during the war

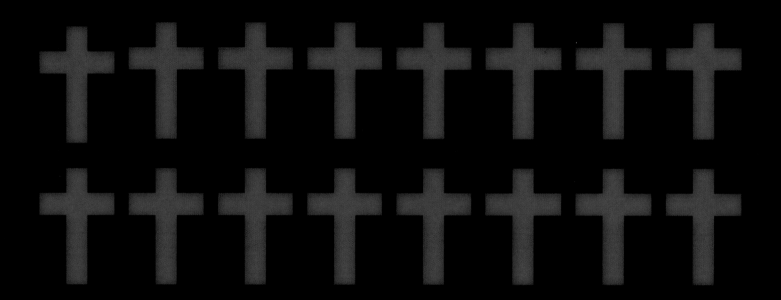

In December 1914 the German Navy bombarded the coastal towns of Scarborough, Hartlepool and Whitby, killing 18 civilians

Casualty numbers (killed and wounded in the navy):

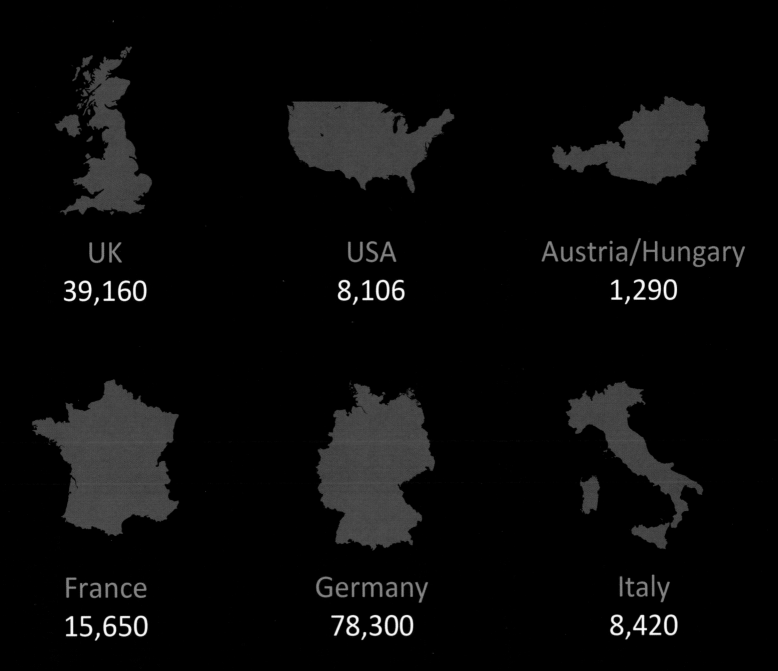

UK
39,160

USA
8,106

Austria/Hungary
1,290

France
15,650

Germany
78,300

Italy
8,420

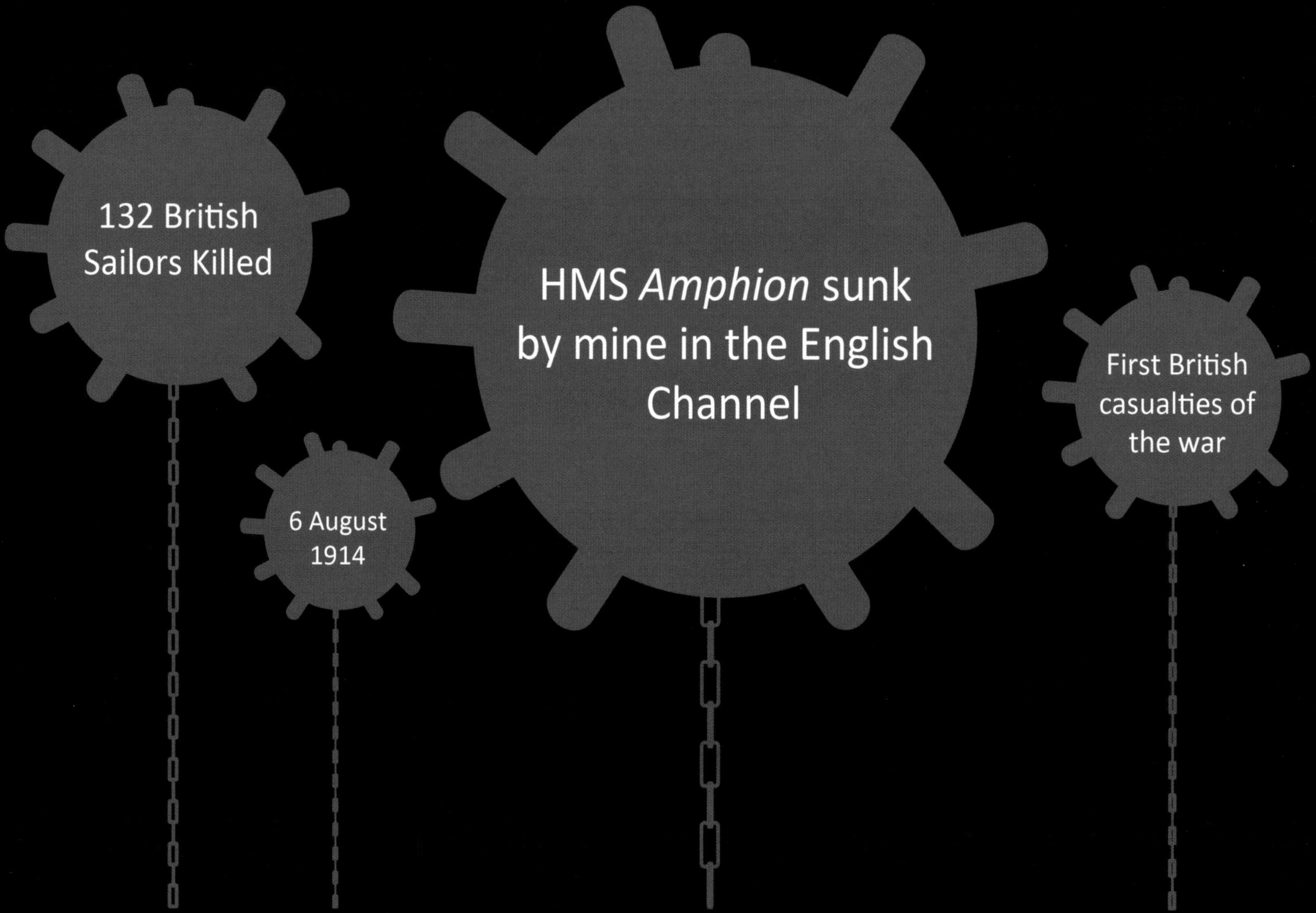
132 British
Sailors Killed
6 August
1914
HMS *Amphion* sunk
by mine in the English
Channel
First British
casualties of
the war

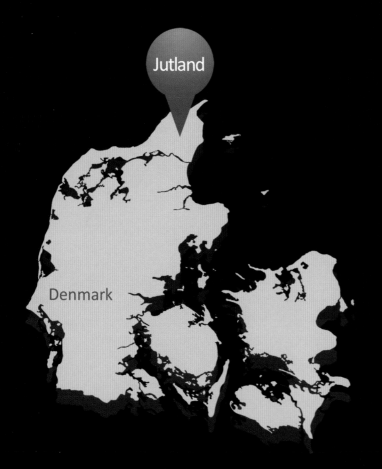

Jutland

Denmark

BATTLE of JUTLAND

31 May – 1 June 1916

The Battle of Jutland was fought in the North Sea near Jutland, Denmark. It was the largest naval battle of the war and the only full scale clash of battleships in the First World War.

British boat losses:

3 battlecruisers   3 cruisers   8 destroyers

German boat losses:

1 battlecruiser   4 cruisers   5 destroyers

'Something wrong with our bloody ships'
During the battle, a salvo struck HMS *Princess Royal*, causing a signalman to wrongly announce that the ship had blown up. Beatty famously replied with 'there seems to be something wrong with our bloody ships today'

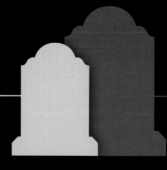

German Casualties
2550

British Casualties
6100

Passenger liner *Lusitania* was sunk by U-20 in May 1915, killing 1,198 people including 128 Americans

HMS *Pathfinder* | 5 September 1914

The first British warship sunk by a U-boat was HMS *Pathfinder*, sunk by a torpedo fired from U-1 near St Abbs Head. She sunk in 4 minutes

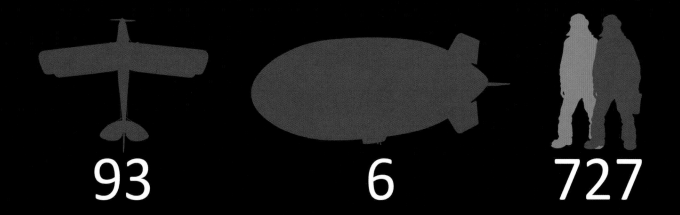

93 **6** **727**

The RNAS had 93 aircraft, 6 airships and 727 staff at the outbreak of war

3,000 **103** **55,000**

By the time it had been amalgamated into the RAF in April 1918, it had 55,000 personnel, 3,000 planes and 103 airships

threehundredseventyfive

375 U-boats were commissioned before the end of the war

U-boat Construction by Year:

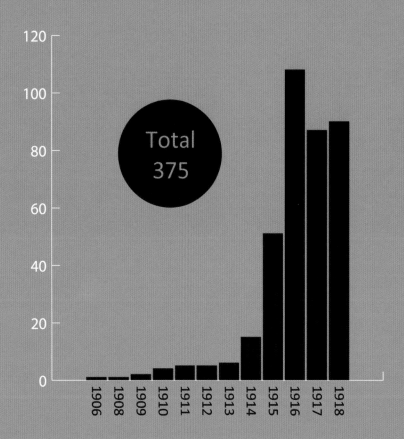

Total
375

10 shipyards built the U-boats

48,158 grt

The largest ship sunk was HMHS *Britannic* which was sunk on 21 November 1916 in the Aegean Sea after hitting a mine laid by U-73. The 48,158-tonne ship sunk in 55 minutes

1750 LIVES

The single biggest loss of life from a U-boat strike was the Italian troopship *Principe Umberto* which was sunk on 8 June 1916 with the loss of 1750 lives

U-35 | 226 Ships Sunk

The most successful U-boat in WW1 was U-35 which sunk 226 ships from 1915 to 1918

Ten Most Successful U-boats (in terms of tonnage sunk)

U-35 | **226 Ships Sunk**

Tonnage Sunk: 538,498 tons

U-39 | **154 Ships Sunk**

Tonnage Sunk: 406,325 tons

U-38 | **139 Ships Sunk**

Tonnage Sunk: 293,124 tons

U-34 | **119 Ships Sunk**

Tonnage Sunk: 257,652 tons

U-53 | **88 Ships Sunk**

Tonnage Sunk: 225,364 tons

U-63 | **73 Ships Sunk**

Tonnage Sunk: 203,418 tons

U-33 | **84 Ships Sunk**

Tonnage Sunk: 194,131 tons

U-64 | **46 Ships Sunk**

Tonnage Sunk: 147,869 tons

U-17 | **98 Ships Sunk**

Tonnage Sunk: 147,154 tons

U-20 | **37 Ships Sunk**

Tonnage Sunk: 145,830 tons

UC Coastal Minelayers (95 built with 3 variations of design)

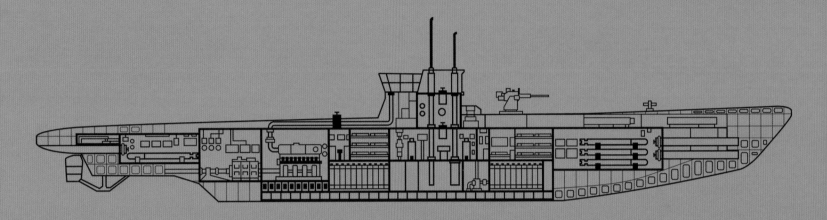

Displacement (tons):	Speed (knots):
417 (sf)	11.6 (sf)
493 (sm)	7.0 (sm)
545 (total)	**Range**
Length (m):	**(miles / knots):**
49.35	9430/7 (sf)
Height (m):	55/4 (sm)
7.46m	**Torpedos:**
Power (hp):	7
500 (sf)	2/1 (bow/stern tubes)
460 (sm)	**Mines:**
	18
	Deck gun:
	88mm
	133 rounds
	Crew:
	14 men
	Max depth:
	50m
	(164ft)

sf = surfaced   sm = submerged

Gasoline Powered Boats (18 built with 8 variations of design)

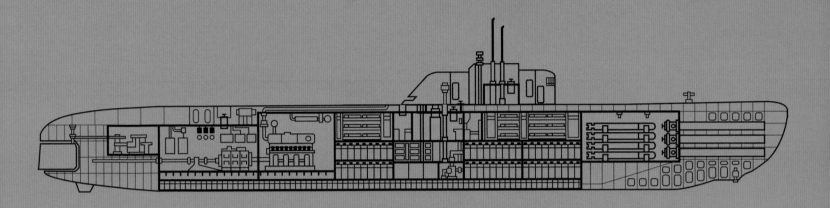

Displacement (tons):	Speed (knots):
493 (sf)	14.2 (sf)
611 (sm)	8.1 (sm)
Length (m):	**Range**
57.38	**(miles / knots):**
Height (m):	3300/9 (sf)
7.05	80/5 (sm)
Power (hp):	**Torpedos:**
1000 (sf)	6
1160 (sm)	2/2 (bow/stern tubes)
	Mines:
	No mines carried
	Deck gun:
	105mm
	300 rounds
	Crew:
	35 men
	Max depth:
	50m
	(164ft)

UE Ocean Minelayers (19 built with 2 variations of design)

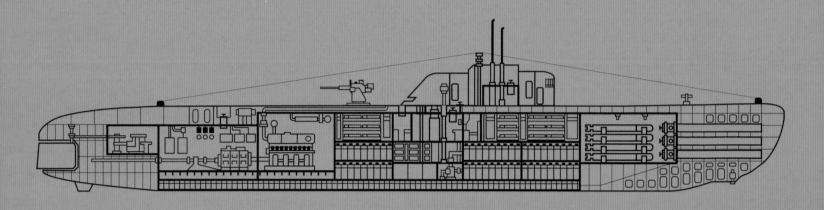

Displacement (tons):	Speed (knots):
755 (sf)	10.6 (sf)
832 (sm)	7.9 (sm)
980 (total)	**Range (miles/knots):**
Length (m):	7880/7 (sf)
56.80	83/4 (sm)
Height (m):	**Torpedos:**
8.25	4
Power (hp):	1/1 (bow/stern tubes)
900 (sf)	**Mines:**
900 (sm)	38
	Deck gun:
	105mm
	130 rounds
	Crew:
	32 men
	Max depth:
	50m
	(164ft)

German Ocean Going, Diesel Powered Torpedo Attack Boats
(18 built with 8 variations of design)

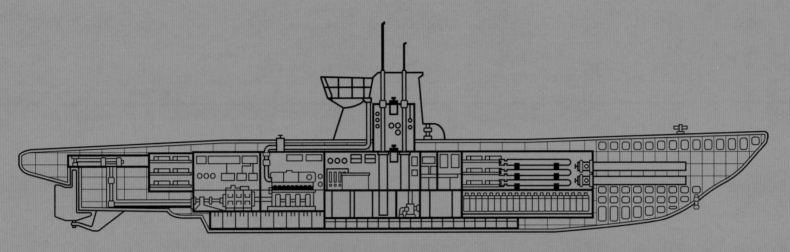

Displacement (tons):	Speed (knots):
685 (sf)	16.4 (sf)
878 (sm)	9.7 (sm)
971 (total)	**Range**
Length (m):	**(miles / knots):**
64.70	8790/8 (sf)
Height (m):	80/5 (sm)
7.68	**Torpedos:**
Power (hp):	6
1850 (sf)	2/2 (bow/stern tubes)
1200 (sm)	**Mines:**
	No mines carried
	Deck gun:
	105mm
	300 rounds
	Crew:
	35 men
	Max depth:
	50m
	(164ft)

UB Coastal Torpedo Attack Boats (136 built with 3 variations of design)

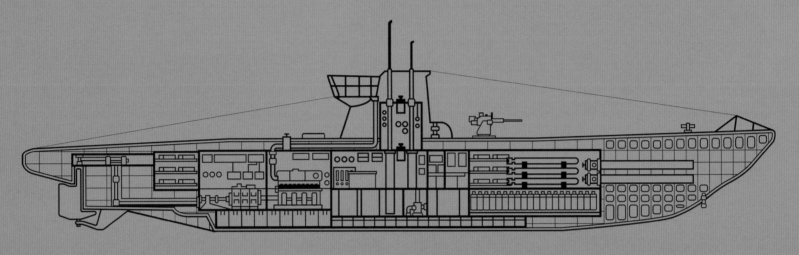

Displacement (tons):	Speed (knots):
516 (sf)	13.6 (sf)
651 (sm)	8.0 (sm)
730 (total)	**Range (miles/knots):**
Length (m):	9040/6 (sf)
55.30	55/4 (sm)
Height (m):	**Torpedos:**
8.25	10
Power (hp):	4/1 (bow / stern tubes)
1100 (sf)	**Mines:**
788 (sm)	No mines carried
	Deck gun:
	88mm
	160 rounds
	Crew:
	34 men
	Max depth:
	75m
	(246ft)

U-Cruisers and Merchant U-Boats (11 built with 3 variations of design)

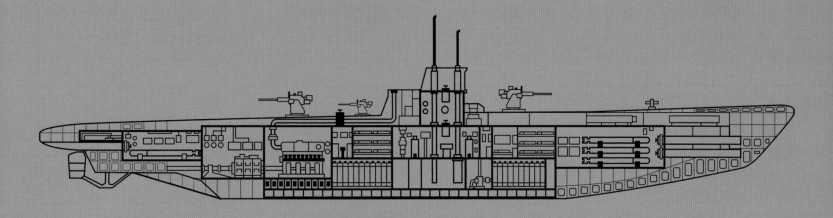

Displacement (tons):	Speed (knots):
1930 (sf)	15.8 (sf)
2483 (sm)	7.6 (sm)
3050 (total)	**Range (miles/knots):**
Length (m):	12630/8 (sf)
92.000 oa	53/4.5 (sm)
71.50 ph	**Torpedos:**
Beam (m):	24
9.12 oa	4/2 (bow / stern tubes)
5.75 ph	**Mines:**
Draught (m):	No mines carried
5.27	**Deck gun:**
Height (m):	2 x 105mm
11.2	980 rounds
Power (hp):	**Crew:**
3300 (sf)	62 men
1780 (sm)	**Max depth:**
	75m
	(246ft)

oa = overall   ph = pressure hull

29 U-boat officers were decorated with the Pour le Mérite

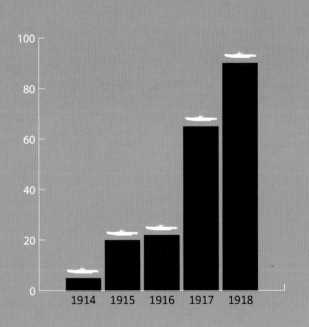

U-boat Losses by Year

Year	Ships
1914	15 ships
1915	755 ships
1916	1516 ships
1917	3718 ships
1918	1642 ships

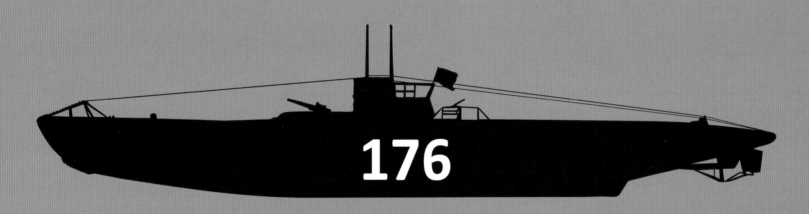

176

As part of the surrender terms, the British Navy received 176 U-boats as spoils of war

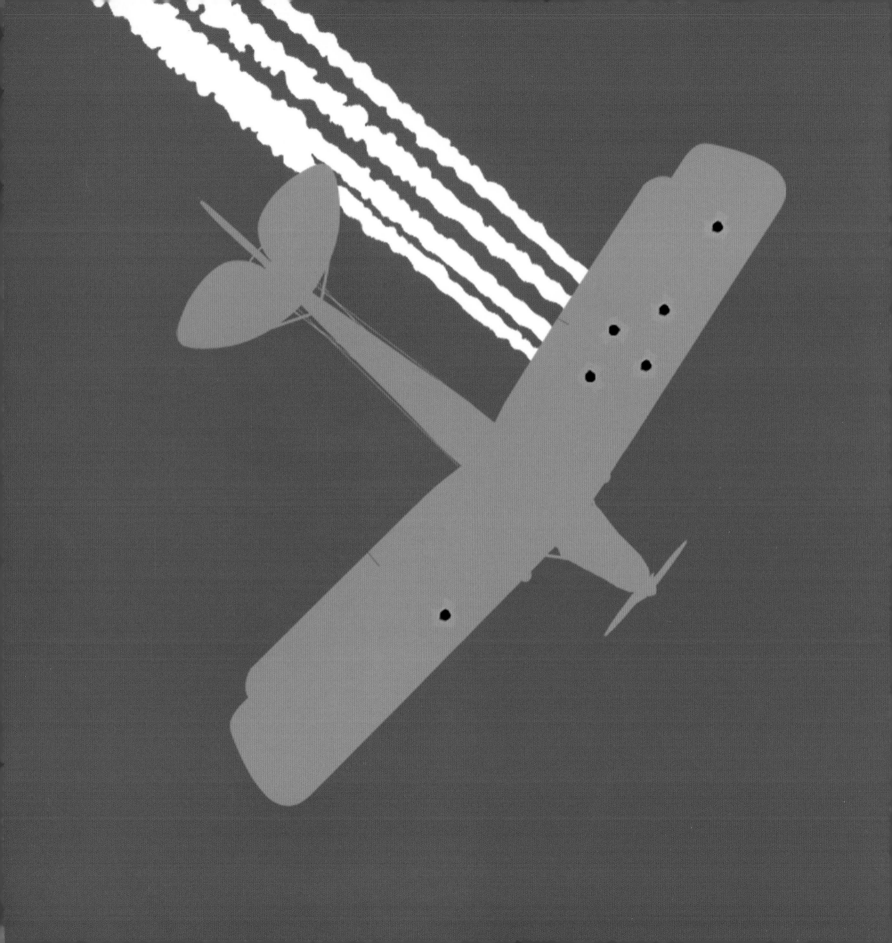

THE WAR IN THE AIR

If there is any aspect of the First World War where innovation, tactics and overall development leapt from advance to advance, it was the war in the air. At the outbreak of war in 1914 man had only been flying for just over a decade. In the beginning the role of aircraft was limited to reconnaissance; however, as the war progressed air forces on all sides took on a much wider and more active role in the hostilities. Fighter planes, bombers, airships and naval aircraft all had a big impact on the war, as did a new phenomenon that appeared from out of the clouds: the fighter ace.

80
Victories

The Red Baron, Manfred von Richthofen scored the highest number of victories in the war – 80.

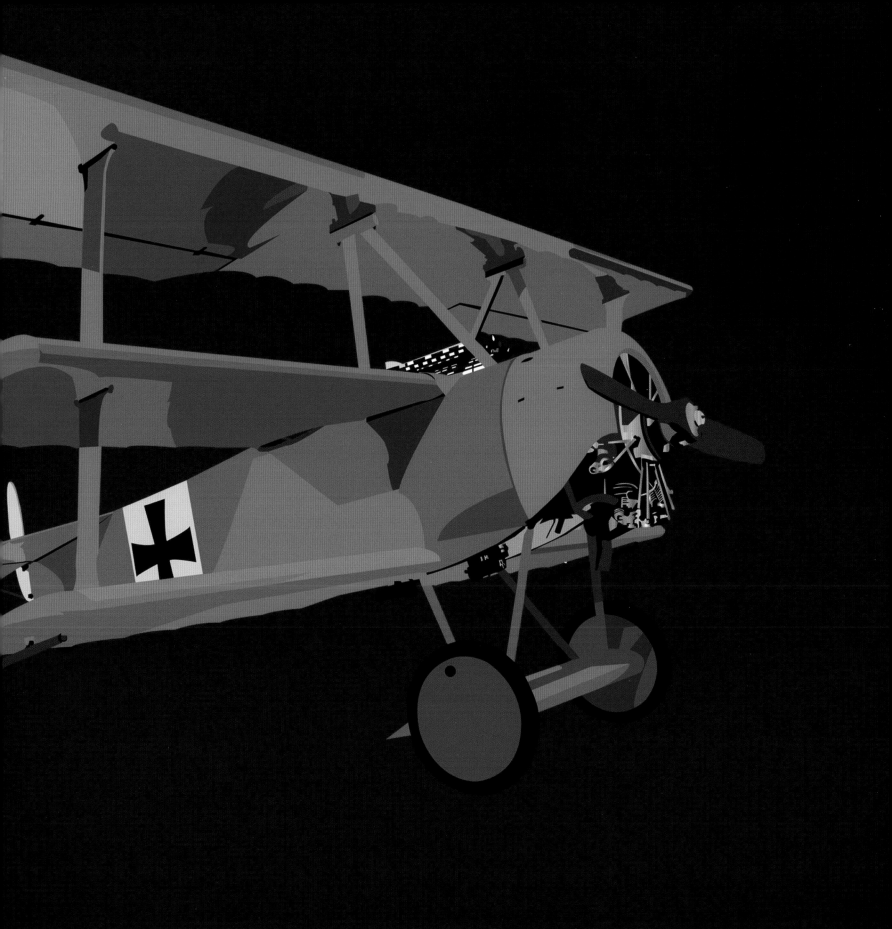

2.2

The number of Allied planes lost for every plane lost by the Central Powers

8,000

8,000 men died in Britain during flight training. More pilots died in accidents than in combat during WW1

20,000

22,000 Canadians served with the RFC and RAF during the war

1,413 civilians were killed by German
Zeppelin and bomber raids on England

During April 1917, the British lost 245
aircraft and 319 aircrew

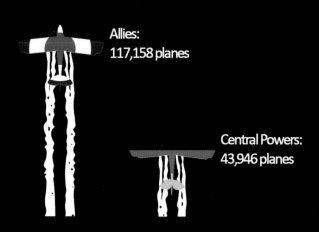

Allied plane manufacturing versus
Central Powers 1914-1918

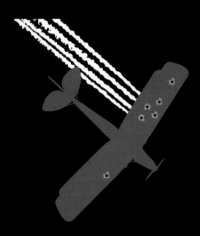

On 1 August 1915, two German pilots
became the first to shoot down another aircraft
using a forward-facing machine gun

To qualify as an ace in the German
Air Force and win the Pour le Mérite medal,
a pilot had to score 8 kills

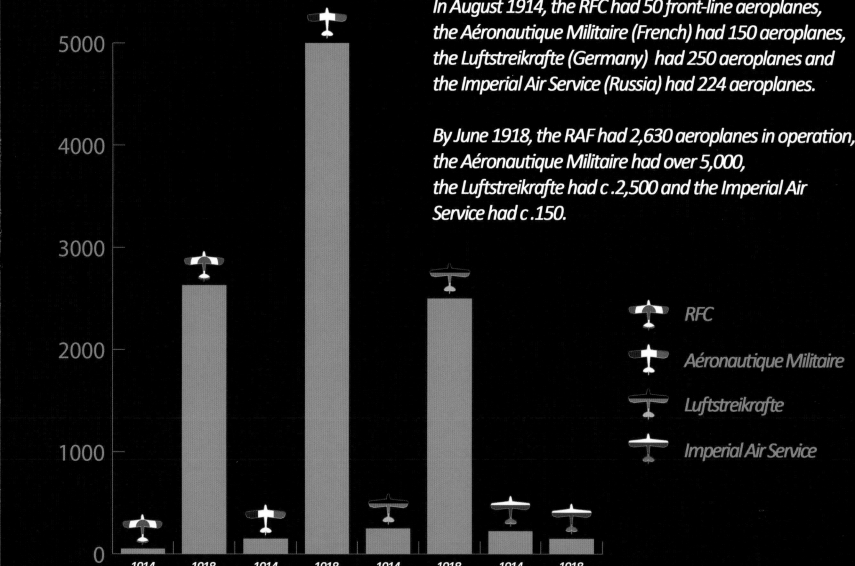

In August 1914, the RFC had 50 front-line aeroplanes,
the Aéronautique Militaire (French) had 150 aeroplanes,
the Luftstreikrafte (Germany) had 250 aeroplanes and
the Imperial Air Service (Russia) had 224 aeroplanes.

By June 1918, the RAF had 2,630 aeroplanes in operation,
the Aéronautique Militaire had over 5,000,
the Luftstreikrafte had c.2,500 and the Imperial Air
Service had c.150.

RFC

Aéronautique Militaire

Luftstreikrafte

Imperial Air Service

5000

4000

3000

2000

1000

0

1914   1918   1914   1918   1914   1918   1914   1918

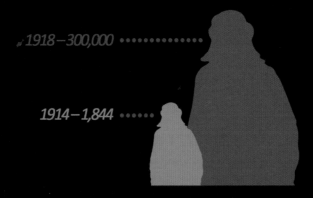

1918 – 300,000

1914 – 1,844

*Total personnel for the RFC in August 1914
was 1,844; by November 1918 it was c. 300,000*

*The RFC (Royal Flying Corps) was
formed in 1912*

*The RAF was formed on 1 April 1918, unifying
the military and naval roles of the RFC and
RNAS into an independent service*

Sopwith Camel

Manufacturer:
Sopwith Aviation Company

Role:
Biplane Fighter

Introduced:
June 1917

Maximum Speed:
115mph

Service Ceiling:
18,000 – 21,000ft

Armament:
2 x .303in Vickers Machine Gun

Number Built:
5,490

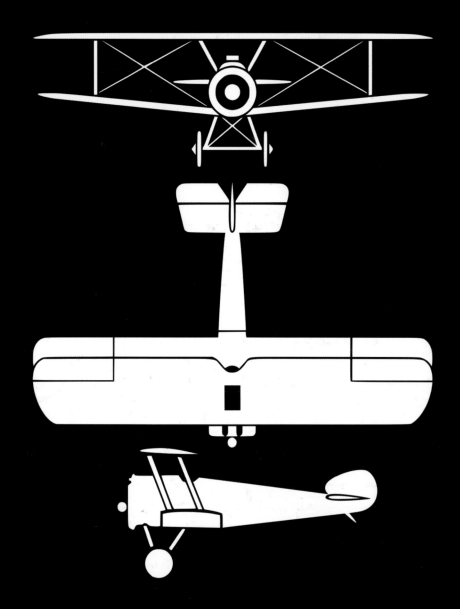

Fokker DR-1

Manufacturer:
Fokker-Flugzeugwerke

Role:
Fighter

Introduced:
July 1917

Maximum Speed:
102mph

Service Ceiling:
20,000ft

Armament:
2 x .312in Spandau Gun

Number Built:
320

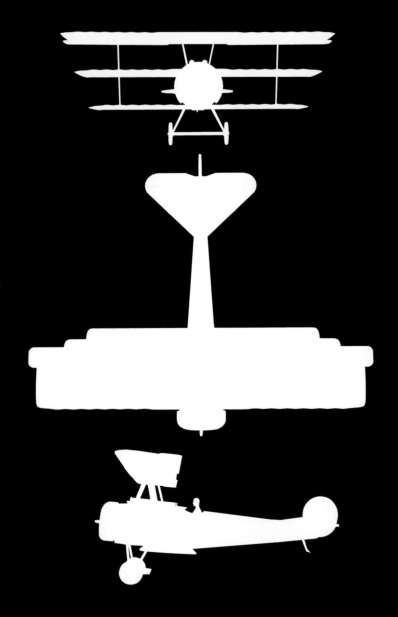

Aircrew Casualties
(Killed/Missing/Wounded)

16,620

7,250

16,050

513

Top 10 Aces of the War

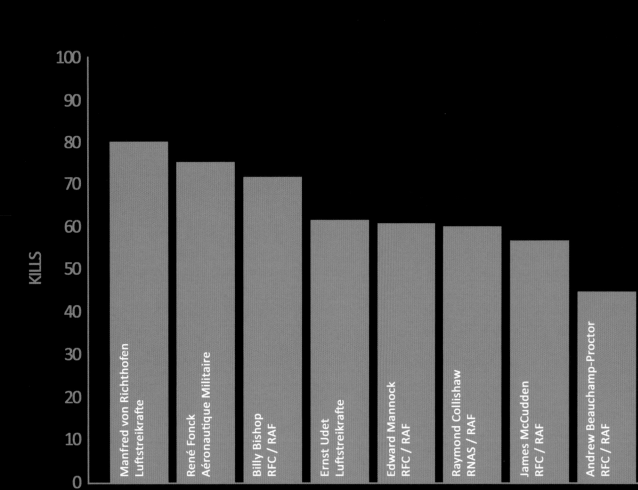

KILLS

100
90
80
70
60
50
40
30
20
10
0

Manfred von Richthofen
Luftstreikrafte

René Fonck
Aéronautique Militaire

Billy Bishop
RFC / RAF

Ernst Udet
Luftstreikrafte

Edward Mannock
RFC / RAF

Raymond Collishaw
RNAS / RAF

James McCudden
RFC / RAF

Andrew Beauchamp-Proctor
RFC / RAF

Erich Löwenhardt
Luftstreikrafte

Donald MacLaren
RFC / RAF

600

The tonnage of British bombs dropped by strategic bombing raids over Germany

7,054

The RFC claimed some 7,054 German aircraft and balloons either destroyed, sent 'down out of control' or 'driven down'

800

During the Battle of the Somme (July – Nov 1916) the RFC lost 800 aircraft and 252 aircrew killed, with 292 tons of bombs dropped and 19,000 recce photographs taken

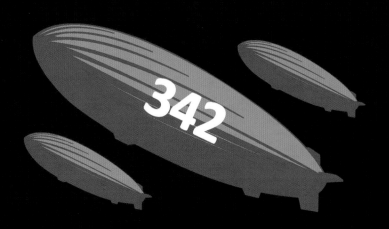

GERMAN AIRSHIPS MADE 342 BOMBING
RAIDS DURING THE WAR

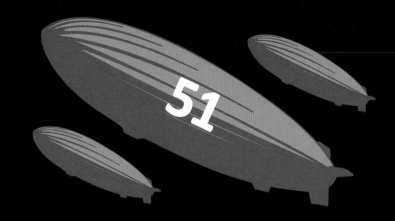

51 OF THOSE RAIDS WERE MADE ON
BRITAIN

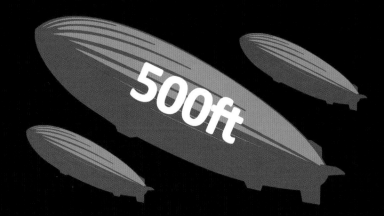

IN 1914 ZEPPELINS WERE 500FT LONG; BY
1916 SUPER ZEPPELINS WERE 650FT

5,806 BOMBS WERE DROPPED ON BRITAIN,
KILLING 557 AND INJURING 1,358

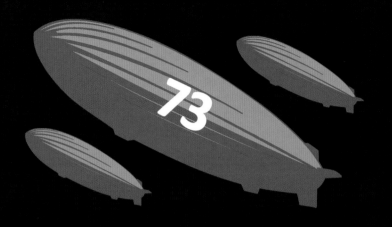

GERMANY OPERATED 73 AIRSHIPS DURING
THE WAR (59 ZEPPELINS)

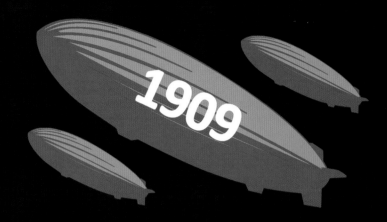

ZEPPELINS FIRST ENTERED MILITARY SERVICE
IN GERMANY IN 1909

elins

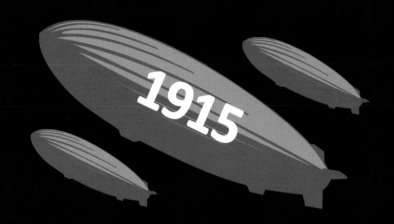

THE FIRST RAID ON ENGLAND WAS 19/20 JANUARY
1915. THE FIRST ON LONDON WAS 31 MAY 1915

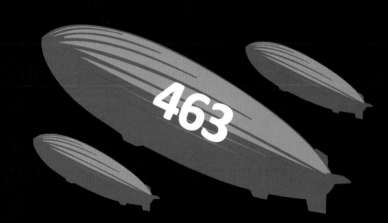

THE BIGGEST RAID ON ENGLAND SAW 463
BOMBS DROPPED BY 14 AIRSHIPS IN SEP 1916

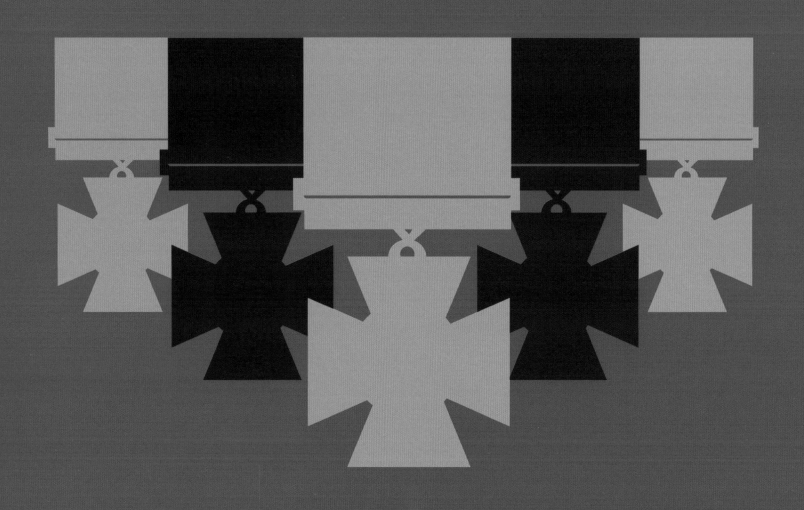

MEDALS

To recognise war service and to reward individual acts of bravery, each of the warring nations issued sets of campaign medals as well as a number of gallantry awards. Some, such as the German Iron Cross and the British Victoria Cross, were already iconic and came to symbolise an entire nation. Other awards, such as the Military Cross and the Distinguished Flying Cross, were brand new and instituted as the war progressed.

The 1914 Star

Instituted: 1917

Campaign: France and Belgium 1914

Number of Medals Issued: approx 378,000

Ribbon: Watered silk with red, white and blue vertical stripes

Metal: Bronze

Size: Height 50mm, width 45mm

Obverse: A four-pointed star topped with a crown, with crossed swords, a central scroll set inside a circular wreath with the royal cypher at its base

Reverse: Plain and flat, inscribed with the recipient's name and service details

Clasp: A bronze clasp inscribed 5th Aug – 22nd Nov 1914 was awarded to those who had been 'under fire' during those dates. A rosette is worn on the ribbon bar

Award Criteria: Awarded to all those who served in land operations on the Western Front between 5 August and 22 November 1914

Notes: Often known as the 'Mons Star'. Although there was fighting elsewhere in 1914, only soldiers who fought on the Western Front were awarded this star. The majority of the recipients were the officers and men of the small professional British Army (BEF)

The 1914–15 Star

Instituted: 1918

Campaign: The First World War 1914–15

Number of Medals Issued: approx 2,350,000

Ribbon: Watered silk with red, white and blue vertical stripes

Metal: Bronze

Size: Height 50mm, width 45mm

Obverse: A four-pointed star topped with a crown, with crossed swords, a central scroll set inside a circular wreath with the royal cypher at its base

Reverse: Plain and flat, inscribed with the recipient's name and service details

Award Criteria: Awarded to all British and Commonwealth forces for service in all theatres, including at sea and in the air, between 5 August 1914 and 31 December 1915, other than those who already had the 1914 Star

Notes: Some 1914 Star recipients were unhappy that the two stars were so visually similar; they wanted a medal that set them apart from their later colleagues

The British War Medal 1914-20

Instituted: 1919

Campaign: The First World War 1914–20

Number of Medals Issued: approx 6,500,000

Ribbon: Watered silk with central orange strip, with strips of white, black and blue

Metal: Silver or Bronze

Size: 36mm

Obverse: An uncrowned profile of King George V

Reverse: St George on horseback trampling over the eagle shield of the Central Powers and the emblems of death

Clasp: None issued although campaign clasps were considered, but the idea scrapped due to the costs

Award Criteria: Awarded to all forces of the British Empire for 'approved' service during the First World War, and to foreign forces who rendered service to the Allied cause, and for service in the Russian Civil War

Notes: Each medal was inscribed around the rim with each recipient's name and service details. Roughly 110,000 medals were issued in bronze and awarded to Chinese, Indian and Maltese personnel in labour corps

The Victory Medal

Campaign: The First World War 1914–20

Number of Medals Issued: approx 5,725,000

Ribbon: A double rainbow with red in the centre and indigo at the edges

Metal: Bronze

Size: 36mm

Obverse: The figure of Victory, holding a palm branch in her right hand and having her left arm outstretched

Reverse: A laurel wreath containing the inscription: THE GREAT WAR FOR CIVILISATION 1914–1919

Award Criteria: Awarded to service personnel who had been awarded the 1914 Star or 1914–15 Star and the majority of service personnel who were awarded the British War Medal

Clasp: None

Notes: Each medal was inscribed around the rim with each recipient's name and service details. It was often known as the Allied War Medal because the same basic design and ribbon was used by 13 other Allied nations. The version issued by the Union of South Africa included reverse text in English and Dutch. The reverse dates are 1914–1919 to include post-war intervention in the Russian Civil War

Memorial Plaque

Instituted: 1919

Campaign: The First World War 1914–18

Number of Medals Issued: approx 1,355,000

Ribbon: None

Metal: Bronze

Size: 120mm

Description: The plaque shows Britannia offering a laurel crown to the name of the recipient. In front of Britannia is a lion and around her shoulder are dolphins. Underneath the lion, a lion cub clutches a fallen eagle. The inscription round the edge of the plaque reads HE (or SHE) DIED FOR FREEDOM AND HONOUR

Award Criteria: Awarded to the next of kin of those who lost their lives on active service, including from wounds, accident or illness, during the war

Notes: Commonly called 'death plaques' or the 'dead man's penny' these plaques were issued along with a parchment scroll. Plaques to women are very rare, with only approx 600 being issued

Silver War Badge

Instituted: 12 September 1916

Campaign: The First World War 1914–18

Number of Medals Issued: approx 1,150,000

Ribbon: None

Metal: Silver

Size: 33mm

Description: A circular pin badge with the crowned royal monogram in the centre and 'FOR KING AND EMPIRE + SERVICES RENDERED' around the edge. Each badge was numbered on the back

Award Criteria: Awarded to service personnel who sustained a wound or contracted sickness which resulted in an early discharge from the war

Notes: This badge was issued to stop men of military age being harassed by women who thought they were avoiding going to the front. One of the women's tactics would be to give the men white feathers

Mercantile Marine War Medal

Instituted: 1919

Campaign: The First World War 1914–18

Number of Medals Issued: approx 133,000

Ribbon: Green and red with a central white stripe, symbolising port and starboard streaming lights

Metal: Bronze

Size: 36mm

Obverse: An uncrowned profile of King George V

Reverse: A scene depicting a merchant ship sailing through rough seas with a sinking submarine in the foreground and a sailing ship in the distance

Clasp: None

Award Criteria: Awarded to members of the Merchant Navy who made at least one voyage within a pre-designated war zone

Notes: Recipients who served solely in the Merchant Navy received this medal plus the British War Medal. Those who served in other units could also qualify for the Victory Medal and the relevant Star if applicable

Victoria Cross (VC)

Instituted: 29th January 1856

Ribbon: 38mm wide. Originally naval crosses used a dark blue ribbon with the army crosses having a crimson ribbon. Since 1918 the crimson ribbon has been used for all awards. The suspension bar is decorated with laurel leaves on the front, on the reverse is engraved the details of the recipient

Metal: Bronze, originally from Russian guns captured in the Crimea, although guns captured in other conflicts have also been used

Size: Height 41mm, Width 36mm

Description: A cross pattée bearing the crown of Saint Edward summounted by a lion, with the words FOR VALOUR inscribed on a semi-circular scroll

Reverse: A circular panel in the centre of the back of the cross in which is engraved the date of the act for which the VC was awarded

Award Criteria: The highest award for gallantry 'in the face of the enemy' available for all ranks in all arms of service. It takes precedence over all other British and Commonwealth orders, decorations and medals

The number of Victoria Cross medals awarded during the First World War by year of award:

1914 — 46 awards

1915 — 117 awards

1916 — 84 awards

1917 — 175 awards

1918 — 207 awards

The number of Victoria Cross medals awarded during the First World War by age of recipient:

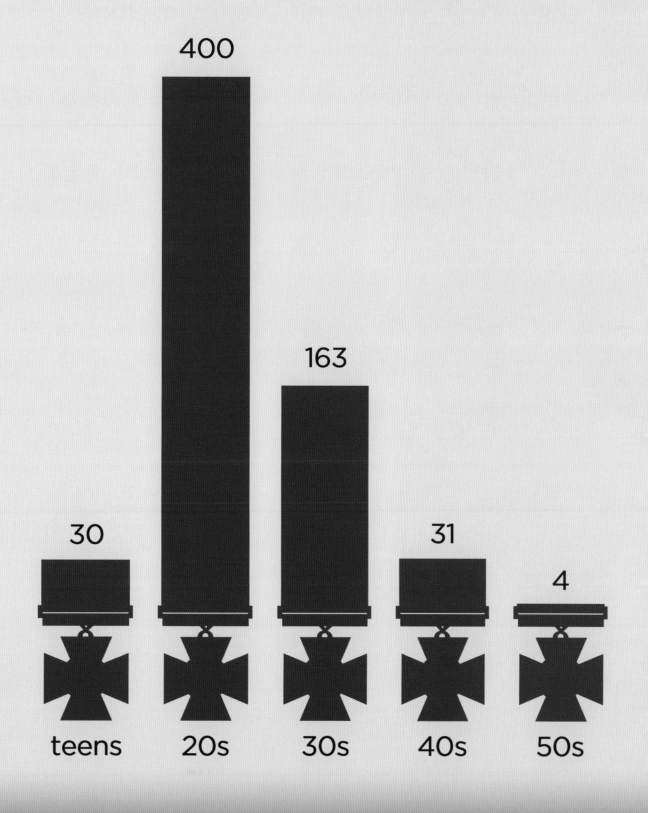

30	400	163	31	4
teens	20s	30s	40s	50s

The number of Victoria Cross medals awarded during the First World War by country:

Britain & Ireland 475

Australia 60

Canada 60

India 18

S. Africa 3

New Zealand 11

Theatres of war with the most VCs awarded:

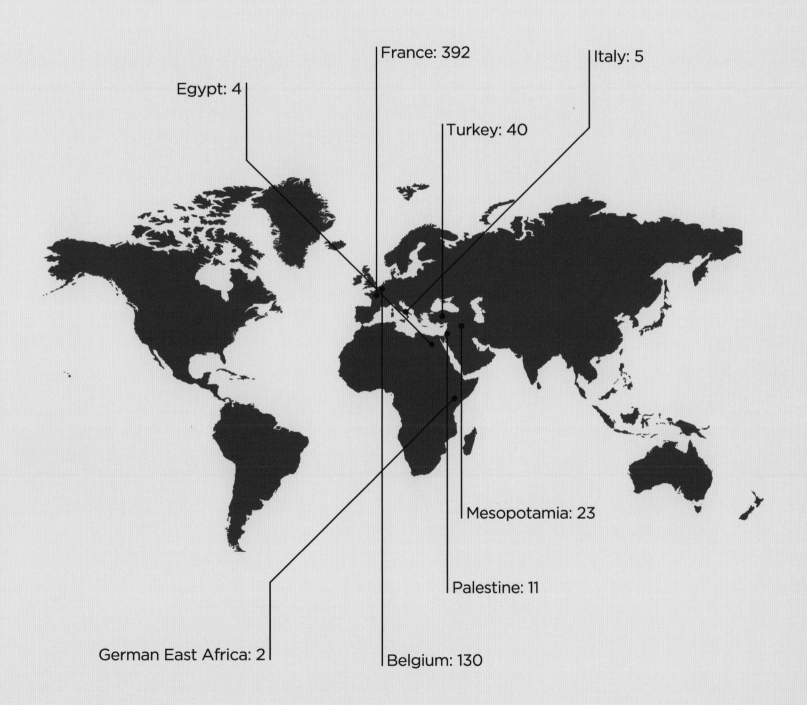

France: 392

Italy: 5

Egypt: 4

Turkey: 40

Mesopotamia: 23

Palestine: 11

German East Africa: 2

Belgium: 130

The number of Victoria Cross medals awarded during the First World War by force:

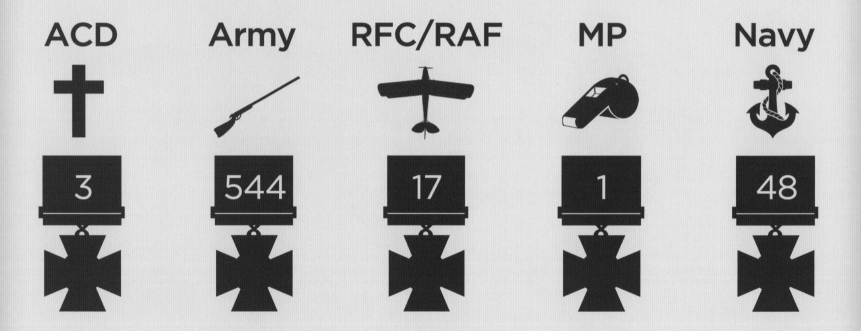

ACD — 3
Army — 544
RFC/RAF — 17
MP — 1
Navy — 48

ACD = army chaplains department   MP = military police

 **First Canadian Winner**

L/Corporal Frederick Fisher
Won at St Julien, France 23 April 1915

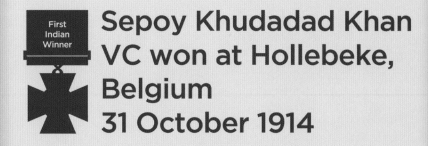 **First Indian Winner**

Sepoy Khudadad Khan
VC won at Hollebeke, Belgium
31 October 1914

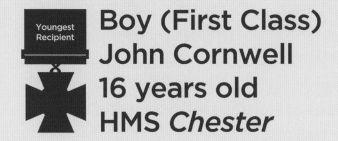 **Youngest Recipient**

Boy (First Class) John Cornwell
16 years old
HMS *Chester*

 **Oldest Recipient**

Marine Master Fred Parslow
59 years old
HMHT *Anglo-Californian*

629

The number of Victoria Cross medals awarded during the First World War

Captain Noel Godfrey Chavasse
Royal Army Medical Corps

9 Aug 1916 Guillemont

31 Jul – 2 Aug 1917 Wieltje

The only person to win 2 Victoria Crosses during the First World War

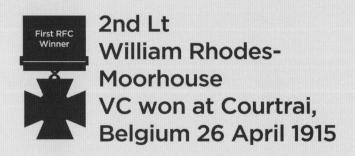

First RFC Winner

2nd Lt William Rhodes-Moorhouse VC won at Courtrai, Belgium 26 April 1915

166

Number of winners who were killed or died of wounds received during their VC action

There is enough bronze left from the captured cannons to make approx 85 more Victoria Crosses

3 men from 1 street in Canada (Pine Street, Winnipeg) were all awarded the VC. CSM Frederick Hall, Corporal Leo Clarke and Lt Robert Shankland. The street was named Valour Road in their honour

Maurice Dease - Sidney Godley - Charles Jarvis - Charles Garforth - Theodore Wright - Ernest Alexander - Francis
Bradbury - George Dorrell - David Nelson - William Johnston - William Fuller Ross Tollerton - George Wilson - E
Hogan - Arthur Martin-Leake - Khudadad Khan - Spencer Bent - John Vallentin - Walter Brodie - John Dimmer - J
William Bruce - Philip Neame - James MacKenzie - Abraham Acton - James Smith - Eustace Jotham - Michael O'L
Fuller - William Anderson - Cecil Noble - Edward Barber - Robert Morrow - Jacob Rivers - George Wheeler - Ge
Bellew - Cuthburt Bromley - Francis Scrimger - Edward Unwin - Richard Willis - Arthur Tidsall - Alfred Richards
Samson - Charles Doughty Wylie - Garth Walford - William Rhodes-Moorhouse - Mir Dast - William Cosgrove
Sharpe - David Finlay - Douglas Belcher - Frederick Barter - Joseph Tombs - John Smyth - Albert Jacka - Marti
Campbell - Walter James - Gerald O'Sullivan - James Somers - Frederick Parslow - Lanoe Hawker - Sidney Woo
Percy Hansen - Alfred Shout - Frederick Tubb - Alexander Burton - William Dunstan - John Hamilton - David
Maling - Frederick Johnson - Harry Wells - Henry Kenny - George Peachment - Kulbir Thapa - Daniel Laidlaw - Ar
Pollock - Edgar Cookson - Alexander Turner - Arthur Fleming-Sandes - Samual Harvey - Oliver Brooks - John R
Bell-Davies - Samuel Meekosha - Alfred Drake - William Young - Alfred Smith - Chatta Singh - John Sinton - Lala
Edgar Myles - James Fynn - Shamamad Khan - Edward Baxter - Charles Cowley - Humphrey Firman - Richard J
Erskine - William Hackett - Arhur Batten-Pooll - William Jackson - James Hutchinson - Nelson Carter - William Mc
Sanders - Robert Quigg - Walter Ritchie - Adrian Carton de Wiart - Thomas Turrall - Thomas Wilkinson - Donald
Blackburn - John Leak - Thomas Cooke - Albert Gill - Claude Castleton - William Evans - James Miller - Willia
John Holland - David Jones - Thomas Hughes - Leo Clarke - John Campbell - Donald Brown - Frederick M
Bradford - Henry Kelly - James Richardson - Hubert Lewis - Robert Downie - Eugene Bennett - Bernard Fre
Murray - Frederick Booth - Frederick Palmer - Gordon Campbell - Thomas Steele - George Wheeler - John Re
Percy Cherry - Frederick Harvey - Joergan Jensen - Frederick Lumsden - William Gosling - James Newland - Th
Waller - Donald MacKintosh - Harold Mugford - John Cunningham - John Ormsby - Charles Pope - Ernest Sy
Brooks - Reginald Haine - Alfred Pollard - James Welch - William Sanders - Robert Combe - John Harrison - Geor
Bishop - Thomas Maufe - John Craig - Robert Grieve - Ronald Stuart - Samuel Frickleton - William Williams -John Ca
Best-Dunkley - Thomas Colyer-Fergusson - Dennis Hewitt - Robert Bye - Alexander Edwards - Ivor Rees - Tom
William Butler - Charles Bonner - Ernest Pitcher - Arnold Loosemore - Thomas Crisp - Michael O'Rourke - Will
Skinner - Frederick Hobson - Montague Moore - Hardy Parsons - Robert Hanna - Filip Konowal - Sidney Day - J
Colvin - William Burman - Alfred Knight - William Hewitt - Walter Peeler - Ernest Egerton - John Hamilton - John
Ockendon - Fred Greaves - Arthur Hutt - Thomas Sage - Joseph Lister - John Molyneux - John Rhodes - William
Holmes - Alexander Lafone - Hugh McKenzie - George Mullin - Cecil Kinross - George Pearkes - John Collins -
Wain - Harcus Strachan - Charles Spackman - Robert MacBeath - Albert Shepherd - John McAulay - George Cla
McReady-Diarmid - George Paton - Stanley Boughey - Gobind Singh - Arthur Lascelles - Henry Nicholas - J
Charles Robertson - Harold Whitfield - Wilfrith Elstob - Manley James - Allan Ker - John Buchan - Edmund de Wir
John Collins-Wells - Frank Roberts - Christopher Bushell - Julian Gribble - Alfred Herring - John Davies - Wi
Oliver Watson - Bernard Cassidy - Stanley McDougall - Gordon Flowerdrew - Alan Jerrard - Theodore Hardy - Pe
Thomas Pryce - James Forbes-Robertson - John Crowe - Jack Counter - Joseph Woodall - Edward Bamford - Alfre
Victor Crutchley - Clifford Sadlier - James Hewitson - George McKean - Robert Cruickshank - William Greg
Joseph Kaeble - Charles Hudson - John Youll - Edward Mannock - Philip Davey - Thomas Axford - Henry Dal
Herbert Miner - John Croak - Jean Brilliant - James Tait - Andrew Beauchamp-Proctor - Thomas Harris - R
Thomas Dinesen - Robert Spallv - Edward Smith - Richard West - Daniel Beak - George Onions - William Joy
Reginald Judson - Henry Weale - Bernard Gordon - William Clark-Kennedy - Cecil Sewellv - James Huffam - G
Alexander Buckley - Claude Nunney - Cyrus Peck - Bellenden Hutcheson - George Prowse - Martin Doyle - Arth
John McNamara - Samuel Needham - Laurence Calvert - Harry Laurent - Alfred Wilcox - David Hunter - Dan
Badlu Singh - John Barrett - Donald Dean - John Gort - Cyril Frisby - Samuel Honey - George Kerr - Thomas Nee
Blair Wark - John McGregor - James Chrichton - Edward (John) Ryan - Robert Gorle - William Merrifield - Frede
Coulson Mitchell - William Holmes - Wallace Algie - Frank Lester - Harry Wood - James Johnson - James McPhie
David McGregor - Francis Miles - Harry Greenwood - Frederick Hedges - William Bissett - Norman Harvey
James Marshall - George Findlay - Arnold Waters - James Kirk - William A

renfell - George Wyatt - Charles Yate Frederick Holmes - Job Drain - Frederick Luke - Douglas Reynolds - Edward
st Horlock - Harry Ranken - Frederick Dobson - Henry May - William Kenny - James Brooke - James Leach - John
n Butler - Thomas Rendle - Darwan Singh Negi - Frank de Pass - Henry Ritchie - Norman Holbrook - Henry Robson
ry - Eric Robinson - Gobar Sing Negi - William Buckingham - Charles Foss - Cyril Martin - Harry Daniels - Wilfred
ge Roupell - Edward Dwyer - Benjamin Greary - Geoffrey Woolley - Frederick Fisher - Frederick Hall - Edward
rank Stubbs - John Grimshaw - George Drewry - Wilfred Malleson - William Keneally - William Williams - George
sy Smith - Edward Boyle - Walter Parker - Edward Warner - John Lynn - John Ripley - James Upton - Charles
asmith - William Mariner - Leonard Keyworth - George Moor - Reginald Warnerford - William Angus - Frederick
ffe - John Liddell - George Boyd-Rochfort - Cyril Bassett - Leonard Keysor - William Forshaw - William Symons
der - Frederick Potts - Hugo Throssell - Wilbur Dartnell - Charles Hull - Arthur Kilby - Anketell Read - George
r Vickers - Angus Douglas-Hamilton - Rupert Hallowes - Arthur Saunders - Robert Dunshire - Alfred Burt - James
es - James Dawson - Charles Vickers - Harry Christian - Thomas Kenny - Gilbert Insall - John Caffrey - Richard
ic McNair - William Cotter - George Stringer - Edward Mellish - Angus Buchanan - Sidney Ware - William Addison
es - Francis Harvey - Edward Bingham - Loftus Jones - John Cornwell - George Chafer - Arthur Proctor - John
dean - Stewart Loudoun-Shand - Lionel Rees - John Green - Eric Bell - Geoffrey Cather - James Turnbull - George
ll - William Congreve - William Boulter - William Faulds - Joseph Davies - Albert Hill - Theodore Veale - Arthur
hort - Gabriel Coury - Noel Chavasse - Martin O'Meara - William Bloomfield - William Robinson - William Allen
ss - John Kerr - Thomas Jones - Frederick Edwards - Robert Ryder - Tom Adlam - Archie White - Roland
rg - John Cunningham - Thomas Mottershead - Edward Henderson - Robert Phillips - Edward Mott - Henry
tt - Jack White - George Cates - Oswald Reid - Archibald Bissett-Smith - Christopher Cox - Frank McNamara
MacDowell - Harry Cator - John Whittle - Ellis Sifton - Thomas Bryan - William Milne - John Pattison - Horace
s - Charles Melvin - John Graham - Arthur Henderson - David Hirsch - Edward Foster - Albert Ball - Edward
Jarratt - George Howell - Michael Heaviside - Rupert Moon - Tom Dresser - Joseph Watt - Albert White - William
ll - William Ratcliffe - John Dunville - Frank Wearne - Frederick Youens - Thomas Barratt - Clifford Coffin - Bertram
yson - Leslie Andrew - James Davies - George McIntosh - Thomas Whitham - Harold Ackroyd - Noel Chavasse
Grimbaldeston - Edward Cooper - Frederick Room - Harry Brown - Wilfred Edwards - Okill Learmonth - John
Carmichael - John Moyney - Thomas Woodcock - Reginald Inwood - Henry Reynolds - Frederick Birks - Hugh
yer - Patrick Bugden - Philip Bent - Lewis Evans - Clement Robertson - Charles Coverdale - Lewis McGee - James
lamp - Frederick Dancox - Clarence Jeffries - Albert Halton - Christopher O'Kelly - Robert Shankland - Thomas
hn Russell - Colin Barron - James Robertson - Arthur Borton - John Carless - John Sherwood-Kelly - Richard
- Neville Elliott-Cooper - Robert Gee - Walter Stone - Samuel Wallace - Cyril Gourley - John Thomas - Allastair
es Emerson - Charles Train - Walter Mills - John Christie - James McCudden - James Duffy - Geoffrey White
- John Sayer - Charles Stone - Reginald Hayward - Ernest Beal - Cecil Knox - Harold Jackson - Herbert Columbine
m Anderson - Alfred Toye - Arthur Cross - Thomas Youngv - Albert Mountain - Basil Horsfall - Alan McLeod
y Storkey - Joseph Collin - John Schofield - Richard Masters - Eric Dougall - Karanbahadur Rana - Arthur Poulter
Carpenter - George Bradford - Arthur Harrison - Percy Dean - Richard Sandford - Norman Finch - Albert McKenzie
William Beesley - Roland Bourke - Geoffrey Drummond - William Ruthven - George Grogan - Joel Halliwell
- Walter Brown - Albert Borella - John Meikle - Richard Travis - Harold Auten - Alfred Gaby - Herman Good
ael Zengel - Frederick Coppinsv - Alexander Brereton - Robert Beatham - Ferdinand West - Percy Statton
- Lawrence McCarthy - Hugh McIver - Samuel Forsyth - David MacIntyre - Harold Colley - Charles Rutherford
ge Cartwright - Edgar Towner - John Grant - Albert Lowerson - William Currey - Robert MacTier - Arthur Hall
Knight - Walter Simpson - William Metcalf - Lawrence Weathers - Jack Harvey - John Young - Walter Rayfield
Burges - Frank Young - William White - Maurice Buckley - William Waring - James Woods - Leonard Lewis
- Thomas Jackson - Milton Gregg - Graham Lyall - Louis McGuffie - Henry Tandy - Bernard Vann - Ernest Seaman
k Riggs - William Johnson - Joseph Maxwell - William Coltman - George Ingram - James Towers - John Williams
Martin Moffat - Thomas Ricketts - John O'Neill - Roland Elcock - Horace Curtis - John Daykins - Alfred Wilkinson
m Barker - William McNally - Wilfred Wood - Thomas Caldwell - Hugh Cairns - James Clarke - Dudley Johnson
y - Adam Archibald - Brett Cloutman - Unknown American Soldier of WW1

Distinguished Service Order (DSO)

Instituted: 6 September 1886

Ribbon: 29mm wide, crimson with dark blue edges

Metal: Silver-gilt

Size: Height 44mm, Width 41.5mm

Description: A cross with curved ends, overlaid with white enamel and edged in gold. Suspended by a swivel ring attached to a laureated bar

Obverse: A green enamel laurel wreath with an imperial crown at its centre

Reverse: Green enamel wreath enclosing the royal monogram

Award Criteria: Awarded for distinguished services during active operations against the enemy

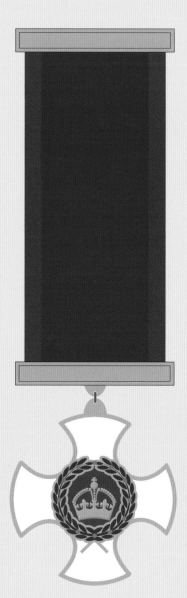

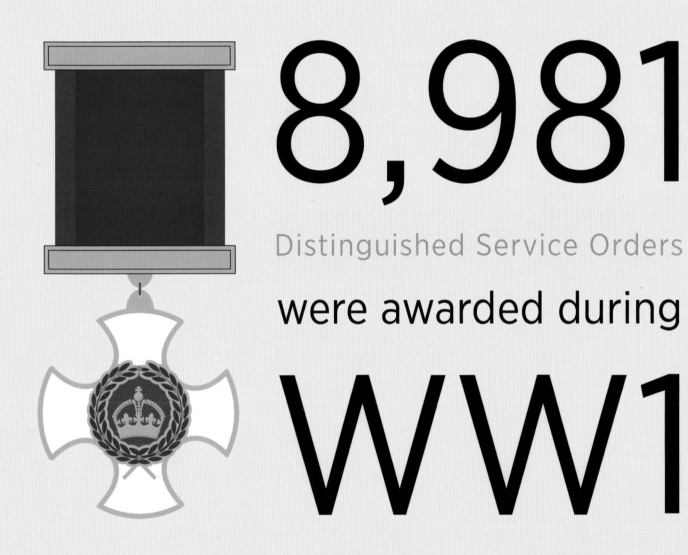

8,981

Distinguished Service Orders

were awarded during

WW1

Multiple awards are denoted by bars ornamented by a crown

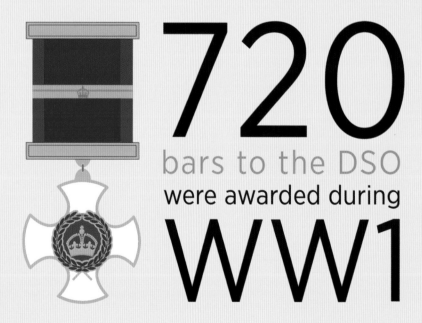

720 bars to the DSO were awarded during **WW1**

75 2nd
bars to the DSO
were awarded during
WW1

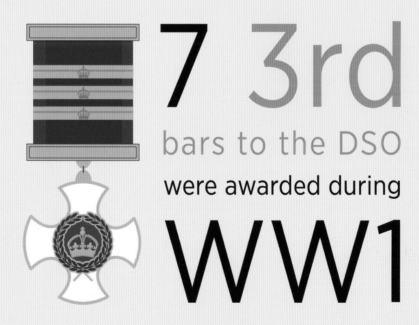

7 3rd
bars to the DSO
were awarded during
WW1

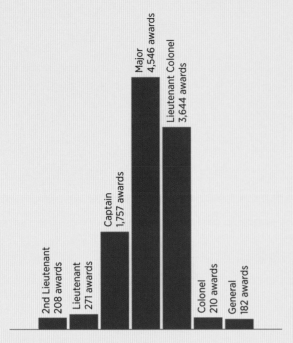

Distribution of rank of DSO recipients during WW1

3,758 of the DSO awards to the British Army came with full citations from the *London Gazette*

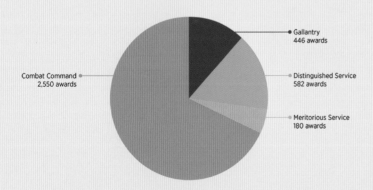

Of the 3,758 DSO awards to officers in the British Army with citations in WW1, 446 were awarded for gallantry, 582 for distinguished service, 180 for meritorious service and 2,550 for combat command

DSO

The recipient of a DSO is known as a Companion of the Distinguished Service Order and is entitled to use the letters DSO after his name

Military Cross (MC)

Instituted: 28 December 1914

Ribbon: 38mm wide with three stripes of white, deep purple, white

Metal: Silver

Size: Height 46mm, Width 44mm

Description: Ornamental silver cross with straight arms terminating in broad finials, suspended from a plain suspension bar

Obverse: Decorated with imperial crowns on each arm, with the royal cypher in the centre

Reverse: Plain

Award Criteria: Awarded for acts of gallantry carried out by junior officers that did not qualify for the VC or DSO

37,081 Military Crosses were awarded during **WW1**

For multiple awards, recipients were given a silver bar with a crown at its centre worn on the ribbon to indicate additional awards

2,995 bars to the MC were awarded during WW1

188 2nd bars to the MC were awarded during **WW1**

04 3rd bars to the MC were awarded during **WW1**

Citations for the MC were published in the *London Gazette*. However, not every MC award came with a citation. Many were awarded as part of the New Year or Birthday Honours lists – these awards were given for continued good service and not one single act of gallantry – and as such no citation was published.

Anyone who was awarded the Military Cross was able to use the letters MC after his name. If they won 2 awards they used MC and Bar after their name.

Distinguished Flying Cross (DFC)

Instituted: June 1918

Ribbon: 30mm original horizontal but after June 1919 diagonal alternative stripes of white and deep purple

Metal: Silver

Size: Height 60mm, Width 54mm

Description: A silver cross flory ending with a rose, surmounted by another cross of propeller blades. The cross is suspended from a bar featuring a sprig of laurel

Obverse: A central roundal with a laurel leaf. The horizontal arms hold wings with the crowned RAF monogram at the centre

Reverse: The royal cypher in the centre with the year of issue engraved on the lower arm

Eligible Recipients: Awarded to commissioned officers and warrant officers of the RAF

Award Criteria: Awarded for acts of valour, courage or devotion to duty performed while flying in active operations

1,116
DISTINGUISHED FLYING CROSSES AWARDED DURING
WW1

A silver slide-on bar was added to the medal ribbon for further acts of valour, for which a subsequent DFC would be awarded

3 AIRMEN RECEIVED A SECOND BAR TO THE DFC IN WW1

THE THREE MEN TO WIN TWO BARS:

Captain Arthur Henry Cobby (Australia – 29 kills)

Captain Walter Hunt Longton (Britain – 11 kills)

Captain Ross MacPherson Smith (Australia – 12 kills)

£36,000

Captain W.H. Longton's medal group was sold at auction for £36,000 in December 2011

CAPTAIN ARTHUR HENRY COBBY

The highest scoring ace in the Australian Flying Corps and the only Australian credited with downing 5 balloons

The Military Medal

Instituted: 25 March 1916

Ribbon: Broad dark blue edges flanking a central white stripe. Within the white stripe are two narrow crimson stripes

Metal: Silver

Size: 36mm

Obverse: Effigy of King George V in full military uniform

Reverse: The crowned royal cypher sits above the inscription FOR BRAVERY IN THE FIELD all enclosed within a wreath

Eligible Recipients: Awarded to Non Commissioned Officers and men of the Army, including the RFC, RAF and Royal Naval Division

Award Criteria: Awarded for individual or associated acts of gallantry and bravery that were deemed not sufficient to merit the Distinguished Conduct Medal

As many as **115,000** Military Medals were awarded during WW1

5,796

Bars to the MM were awarded during WW1

180

Second Bars
were awarded
during WW1

Ernest Albert Corey
Military Medal & 3 Bars
Australian Imperial Force

The only soldier to win
the Military Medal
on four occasions

Dorothie Feilding, a volunteer nurse and motor ambulance driver, was the first woman to be awarded the Military Medal on September 1916

Iron Cross 1st Class
*Worn on the left side of the
recipient's uniform using a pin
or pair of screw posts*

In 1813, 1870 and 1914, Iron Crosses had three grades:
Iron Cross 2nd Class, Iron Cross 1st Class
and Grand Cross of the Iron Cross

Grades

Iron Cross 2nd Class
Suspended from a black and white ribbon instead of pinned to the uniform

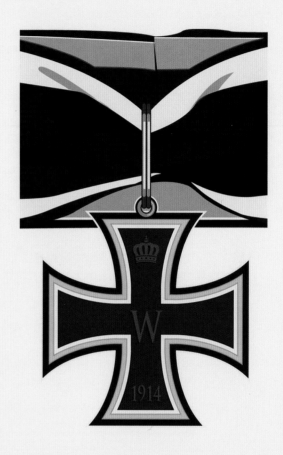

Grand Cross of the Iron Cross
Suspended from a black and white ribbon instead of pinned to the uniform

The Iron Cross 1st Class and the Iron Cross 2nd Class were awarded without regard to rank.
One had to possess the 2nd Class in order to receive the 1st Class

Grand Cross of the Iron Cross

The were only 5 awards of the Grand Cross of the Iron Cross during WW1:

* Kaiser Wilhelm II
* Paul von Hindenburg, later elevated to the Star of the Grand Cross of the Iron Cross
* Erich Ludendorff
* Prince Leopold of Bavaria
* August von Mackensen

The Iron Cross

Established by King Friedrich Wilhelm III of Prussia and first awarded on 10 March 1813 during the Napoleonic Wars

It was annotated with the year indicating the era in which it was issued. For example, an Iron Cross from the First World War bears the year 1914

During the First World War, approximately 218,000 EKIs, 5,196,000 EKIIs and 13,000 non-combatant EKIIs were awarded

EKI = (Eisernen Kreuz) Iron Cross First Class
EKII = (Eisernen Kreuz) Iron Cross Second Class

Order Pour le Mérite (Blue Max)

Known informally as the 'Blue Max', the Pour le Mérite is the highest order of merit issued by the Kingdom of Prussia

Instituted in 1740 by King Frederick II of Prussia, it has a French name because that was the leading language of the Prussian court at the time

A blue enamelled Maltese Cross with golden eagles between the arms. On the body of the cross are the Prussian royal cypher and the words Pour le Mérite written in gold letters. The order is worn at the neck and has a wide black and white striped ribbon: the colours of Prussia

Pour le Mérite awards in the First World War (Total: 687)

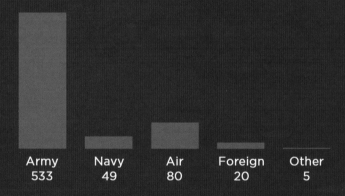

Army	Navy	Air	Foreign	Other
533	49	80	20	5

First Award:
General von Emmich
7 August 1914

The first Pour le Mérite to be awarded during the war was to General von Emmich on 7 August 1914. It was given in honour of his leadership role in the battle to neutralise Liege fortifications

For airmen to be awarded the Blue Max they had to shoot down 8 enemy aircraft. This was increased to 16 by early 1917 and to 30 by the end of the war

Last Award:
Theo Osterkamp
2 September 1918

The last Pour le Mérite to be awarded during the war was to flying ace Theo Osterkamp on 2 September 1918.

The order could not be awarded posthumously. Many awards had to be cancelled because the would-be recipient died while the paperwork was being drawn up

The Medal of Honor

First established in 1861, the Medal of Honor is the United States of America's highest military award. It is awarded for personal acts of valour above and beyond the call of duty

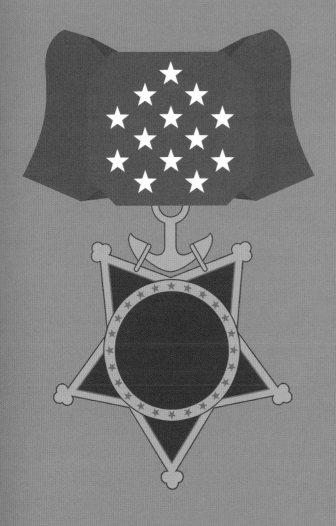

During WW1 there were two varieties of the Medal of Honor: one for the Navy and one for the Army

THIRTEEN

Gunnery Sergeant Robert Guy Robinson was shot 13 times during a dogfight over Belgium on 14 October 1918. Despite this he fought off 12 enemies before returning to base

119 men received the Medal of Honor for their actions during the war

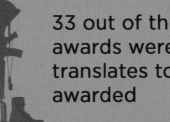

33 out of the total 119 Medal of Honor awards were posthumous. This translates to 27.7% of all medals awarded

CASUALTIES OF WAR

The casualty toll of the First World War is beyond comprehension to modern civilians. It is easy to become numb to the scale of loss when all you see are numbers on a page. Britain alone lost over 1 million dead, but it wasn't just the huge numbers of killed soldiers; millions more were wounded, many were grievously maimed for life and many more were psychologically scarred with conditions such as shell shock. It wasn't just human casualties either: thousands of horses, mules, pigeons and dogs served at the front in various roles. They also suffered terrible losses as they tried to serve their masters as best they could.

There were **35,000,000** casualties

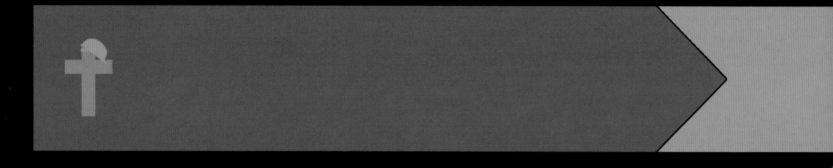

15,000,000 dead

0%

(killed / wounded) during WW1

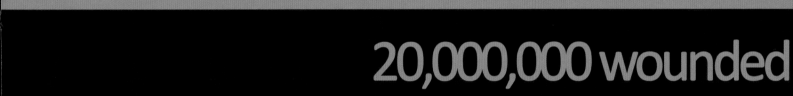

20,000,000 wounded

100%

66% of all military deaths were in battle – as opposed to earlier conflicts where disease and illness killed more than actual fighting

WW1 Death Summary

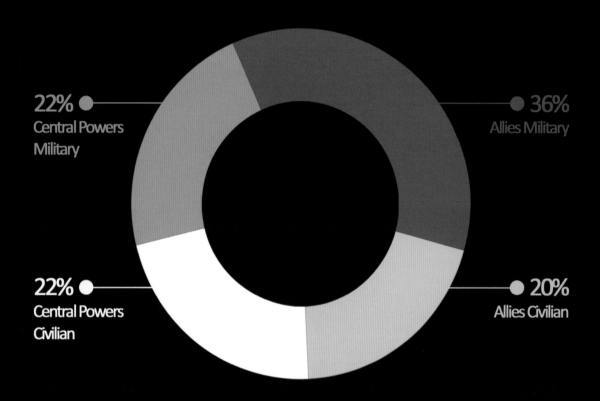

22% ● Central Powers Military

36% ● Allies Military

22% ● Central Powers Civilian

20% ● Allies Civilian

Central Powers Military   Allies Military

Central Powers Civilian   Allies Civilian

WW1 Death Rate

During WW1, **230** soldiers perished for
each hour of the four and a quarter years it continued

Allied Death Summary

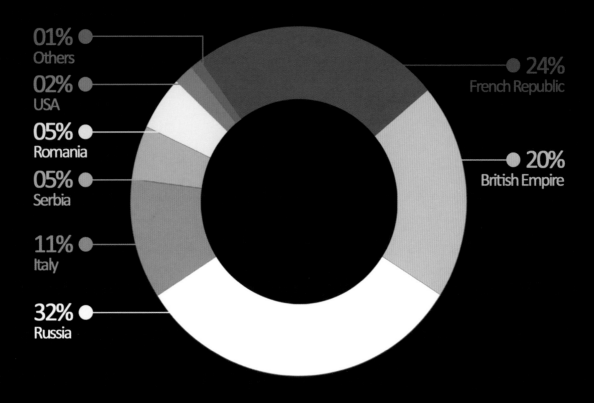

01% Others
02% USA
05% Romania
05% Serbia
11% Italy
32% Russia

24% French Republic
20% British Empire

Others | Romania | Italy | British Empire
USA | Serbia | Russia | French Republic

Central Powers Death Summary

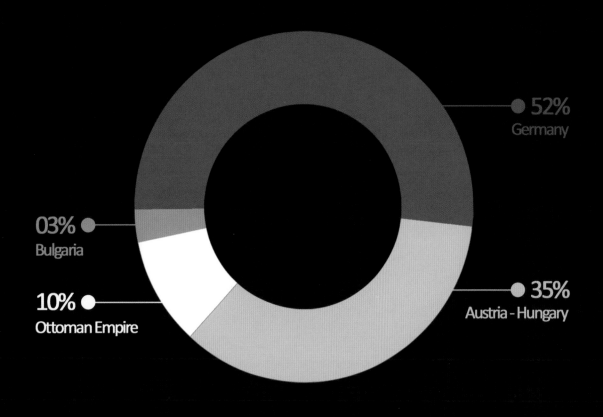

52%
Germany

35%
Austria - Hungary

03%
Bulgaria

10%
Ottoman Empire

Bulgaria   Germany

Ottoman Empire   Austria - Hungary

British Amputees

At the end of the war there were **250,000** wounded
British soldiers who suffered total or partial amputation

Train Deaths

In December 1917 in France, over **600** soldiers died in the world's worst ever train accident

First Day Of The Somme

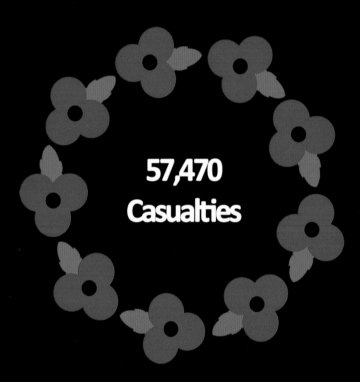

57,470
Casualties

Britain lost **57,470** casualties (killed and wounded) on the first day of the Battle of the Somme

The Battle Of Verdun

1,000,000 Casualties

The Battle of Verdun in 1916 caused **1,000,000** casualties (approx), about half of which were killed

British Casualties

Of all British soldiers mobilised, **33.67%** were killed or wounded

Unknown Graves

7,500,000 soldiers who died in WW1 have
no known grave

French Casualties

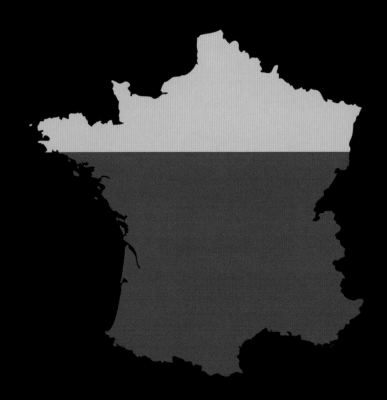

Of all French soldiers mobilised, **67.9%** were killed or wounded

French Casualties Continued

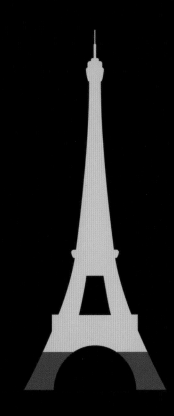

During the course of WW1 **11%** of France's
entire population was killed or wounded.

ARMISTICE AND REMEMBRANCE

The history of the First World War can be read on grave markers and memorials across the world. After the final armistice was signed by Germany on 11 November 1918, the time came for all sides to think about how best to remember their fallen heroes. Cemeteries were built along all of the fighting fronts and thousands of local memorials were erected in towns and villages across Europe. In 1922, as he visited some of the war graves along the Western Front, King George V commented, 'I have many times asked myself whether there can be more potent advocates of peace upon earth through the years to come, than the massed multitude of silent witnesses to the desolation of war.'

11th **Hour**
Month
Day

The fighting was to officially end at 11am on 11 November 1918

3

There were 3 separate armistices signed towards the end of WW1:
- Turkey signed an armistice on 30 October 1918
- Austria-Hungary signed an armistice on 3 November 1918
- Germany signed an armistice on 11 November 1918

30 DAYS

The original peace treaty with Germany was valid for 30 days, but was continually renewed until the signing of the Treaty of Versailles

27

27 victorious powers signed the Treaty of Versailles

226 BILLION REICHMARKS

Size of the reparations imposed on Germany by the Allies

863

British and Commonwealth deaths on 11 November

**Believed to be
the last British battle
casualty of the war:**

**L/12643 Private George Ellison
5th (Royal Irish) Lancers
Died on 11 November 1918, aged 25 years old**

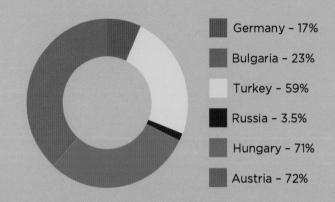

Germany – 17%

Bulgaria – 23%

Turkey – 59%

Russia – 3.5%

Hungary – 71%

Austria – 72%

**The percentage of land (square mile of total pre-war empire)
lost after the war**

**There are 203 WW1 German military cemeteries in France, Belgium
and Luxembourg**

**There are 372 WW1 Commonwealth War Graves Commission (CWGC)
cemeteries in Belgium and 1,620 in France**

**The largest CWGC
cemetery is**

Tyne Cot, Belgium

11,956

**Commonwealth servicemen
buried or commemorated**

**The largest memorial
to the missing:**

Thiepval Memorial

72,116

**Names of soldiers with no
known grave**

THE GREAT W

8,300,000
OFFICERS & MEN KILLED

19,500,000
WOUNDED

LEST WE

AR 1914-1918

7,000,000
MAIMED FOR LIFE

8,000,000
CIVILIANS KILLED

FORGET

FIRST WORLD WAR CENTENARY

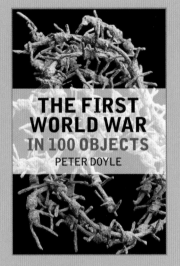

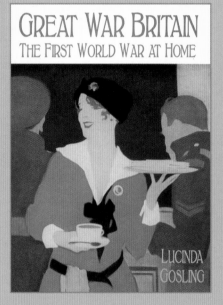
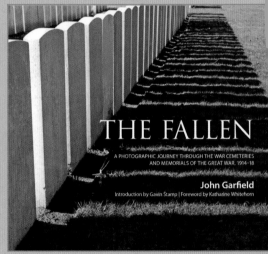

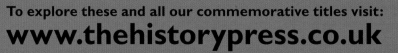